Labyrinth of Deceit and Betrayal

Index:

Page

Dedication

This work is dedicated to hero's who won our liberties at war

Fourth Estate protectors - George Lee – Charlie Bird – RTE-Ireland

Corruption Breakers- Karl Flinders and Rebecca Thomson-UK Computer Weekly

Rule Britannia- Sir Alan and Lady Suzanne Bates, UK ITV and the J.F.S.A

Victims of oppression - Justice Crusaders

Those who were beaten

Those who have been lost

Our A team

The burning question about the "Labyrinth of Deceit and Betrayal" is Why Now?

It is 2024 and the Horizon computer program was introduced in 1999 in the UK. The Eatwells were evicted from their farm in Franz Josef in 1999.

For anyone who has watched the ITV series Mr Bates Vs the Post Office, and felt the pain of the victims of the UK Post Office's callous tactics to break them; you will understand why.

As time passes most grief we feel will heal, or at least the pain dampens down, but the depressing pain of injustice actually gets worse as time goes by and dotage sets in.

Sir Alan Bates told the inquiry into the UK Post Office scandal that he "dug his heals in" because he couldn't bear to think the "baddies would get off scot free", while Karl Flinders of the UK Computer Weekly said "It's so frustrating watching those with power and influence trample on people unchallenged."

Viewing the ITV drama made me realize that it is very important for New Zealanders to know the truth about how few natural rights they have to protect them if they ever come under the attack of the lawless corporates when they wield their power of money against you.

In this story many public officials and MP's have been approached seeking help; some of whom are no longer with us; however anybody named in this book have only been identified because they were instrumental and/or associated with the events involved.

The express intention is to record the history of the deceit and betrayal that has manifested in the State being found deficient in its human rights obligations as a signatory to United Nations Human Rights laws.

The message to any person who feels aggrieved in any way from the history recorded within this "Labyrinth of Deceit and Betrayal," is that I respectfully suggest they fact check what has been written.

We all have to live with our own conscience.

The "Labyrinth of Deceit and Betrayal" has been written in the third person in a deliberate effort to make the subject matter accessible to as many people as possible.

Questions asked of the reader throughout this book are intended to allow you to form your own opinion of the situations and/or scenarios that are being questioned.

Prologue/ History:

"Labyrinth of Deceit and Betrayal" has been written with the objective to record the history of the struggles that constitute a gross miscarriage of justice in New Zealand that has been cast aside by every level of authority in New Zealand involving Prime Ministers, Cabinet Ministers, Government Officials, and Offices of compliance and Members of Parliament for more than 20 years. The power of money has hidden the same foul executive culture exposed by the inquiry into the UK Post Office scandal, as being the common practices applied by New Zealand's corporates and officials.

The first director of the Serious Fraud Office, Charles Sturt said that in his first 4 years that out of 41 cases successfully prosecuted 18 of them involved people who were not aware they had been defrauded. At that time the SFO director was proud to say that the success was due to the proactive policy that had "contributed significantly to the true worth of the SFO".

Facts of the events recorded in this book demonstrate that the SFO obviously abandoned the "proactive policy" when Charles Sturt left the office and now the enforcement agency fails to investigate a fraud even when a victim of fraud provides prima facie' evidence of a complex crime to them.

The vile executive practices experienced can only be described as totally inhuman and barbaric, but the denial of natural justice caused by the inability of elected Members of Parliament to uphold the fundamental Human Rights obligations of the State is a total betrayal of all those who fought wars with the belief that we could live in a just society.

With the memory of the fallen in mind we view the witness statements being recorded at the official inquiry into the UK Post Office scandal with shame. The detail of the evidence being uncovered in the inquiry is showing glaring parallels to oppression reported in New Zealand, while the disgraceful performance of the defective processes of Government fail to protect citizens under International Human Rights law to which the State is a signatory.

The history of the events recorded in this book have been derived from emails, correspondence, Hansard records and other official and public information that has provided the facts of the injustices exposed.

There are several references to the BCAC which is the (Bank Customer Action Collective) that was a support group set up by Suzie Edmonds, (Gray's sister) Vickie & Gray Eatwell and other citizens affected by a Bankers draconian tactics. While the reference to EUFA (Exposing Unacceptable Financial Activities), was set up by Gray and Suzie along with some of the victims of the scandalous finance company collapses, to combine with others to speak up for the beleaguered investors rights. The facts show an inherent political betrayal of the core principles of justice that democratic British Commonwealth States are signatory to as members of the United Nations.

Chapter 1

De'ja' Vu

While visiting family in New Plymouth in April 2024 we were alerted to the ITV series Mr Bates Vs the Post Office being screened on TVNZ, when our sister in law said "you just have to watch this program, it is exactly the same as the battle you had with the BNZ".

She said in a way that only Jenny does "you are retired — so now you have time to finish the job." So we sat down the next two evenings and watched the 3 episodes of the ITV drama and the documentary of Mr Bates Vs the Post Office in the UK.

The first episode wasn't far through when Jenny said "Look at Alan Bates he didn't give up did he, and he found the computer problem way back in 1999, a bit like you."

The story was giving me a strong feeling of De'ja' Vu seeing how the isolated and frightened individual Sub Postmasters were being persecuted by the vile tactics of the Post Office executives and the management systems. The well-acted emotions of Jo Hamilton when she had rung the help line about the inaccuracies she had found in her accounts, turned to fear and panic when the screen changed before her eyes, her expression of horror went right through me and bought back some of the deep feelings of depression that I have lived with since the late 1990's. The panic of Lee Castleton and his disbelief was just like a young man we had witnessed when the BNZ had taken his family business down under very dubious circumstances. The disgrace and embarrassment felt by Saman Kaur and his wife was so familiar to my family and many other individuals suffering from the draconian actions of their bankers, and we were shunned by the community, friends and colleagues in the same way.

It was unnerving to see how Michael Rudkin's wife was crushed to shut him up from exposing the truth of the known problems of the IT system that he had learned from the Horizon operator he had visited at the call centre. The oppressive actions taken against Michael Rudkin by attacking his sub Postmaster wife was so typical to the way people who complain about a bankers practices in New Zealand are treated.

The problem is that a bank takes exception to customers who report any wrongdoing they discover in their bank statements, pretty much the same as how the UK Post Office reacted to Alan Bates and his group when they reported the faults in the Post Office's computer program.

The comparison between the UK situation and our own experience is that all Alan Bates did to upset the Post Office was to find a problem in the computer program and insist they fix it and all we did was complain when we discovered that our bank had been secretly taking money out of our bank accounts and asked them to fix it.

On both sides of the globe they didn't know how to fix it, so they did what corporates do, just get rid of the complainants. Attack the person and the problem will go away.

That's what they thought.

The problem Alan Bates exposed, has led to a cruel travesty that is being hailed as the greatest miscarriage of justice in the history of the British legal system.

The ITV drama has shown the foul tactics that were imposed on the Sub Postmasters who were wrongly accused of theft which saw hundreds of good people thrown in jail to cover up the fact that the Post Office hierarchy had purchased the Horizon computer system that was proving to be faulty.

As we watched the inhuman way the Post Office executives had treated these totally innocent and confused individuals, it really did stir up that horrible empty feeling of betrayal in my gut.

It was very hard to watch how the corporate system has fought Alan Bates, but satisfying to see how his determination and tenacity has led to the victims finally having the disgraceful criminal records quashed after their 23 + year battle.

Witnessing the current inquiry into the scandal makes it very hard to comprehend how such a horrible corporate culture can be accepted in the land that promises the protection of the rule of law to all people, particularly while the mandated authorities turned a blind eye and ignored the atrocities that have been endured by so many for so long. To add insult to injury many of the management personnel and lawyers involved deliberately mislead officials to defeat the truth for many years.

It has taken over 23 years for the Government of the United Kingdom to finally pass legislation to pardon the wrongly accused and convicted Sub Postmasters.

In New Zealand we have been born and bred believing in democracy and the sanctity of living in the free world, and ever since people born in the baby- boomer years have been taught to honour the British Commonwealth and the British Monarchy, and most of us did.

Having been bought up during the years following the Second World War we would always stand to attention to

God Save the Queen, hats were removed in respect, whenever the national anthem was played at school assembly, movies and other public functions.

The Parliamentary system in New Zealand was founded on the Westminster system as a member of the British Commonwealth and New Zealand is a signatory to the same United Nations Declarations of Human Rights and other societal standards of the United Nations.

Therefore it seems quite fitting that the current inquiry into the UK Post Office scandal is being held in Westminster.

New Zealanders born in the years immediately after the end of the Second World War mostly had fathers; grandfathers, mothers and other extended family who fought in or had their lives put on hold by the war.

They willingly did without many basic necessities for what they called the war effort.

Many thousand young New Zealanders were killed and maimed along-side the British Services in the two world wars, and many others came home with horrible injuries that affected them for the rest of their lives. My own Grandfather suffered for his whole life from the injuries he received in the trenches of France in the First World War. He was a stretcher bearer, but unfortunately he was seriously wounded on 5th

April 1918 when out in the muddy fields at the Somme helping a wounded soldier, but he was eventually sent home on the hospital ship SS Ampton sailing for home on 31st July 1918.

All of his life our Grand-Pop suffered from shell shock which I believe had a direct impact on his whole family, as we grew up I watched the depressing emotional effects on my father and my aunties, who lived with depression for their whole life. I believe that as young children they were seriously impacted from the chilling fear of hearing the blood curdling screams of their father during frequent episodes of night mares and when he suffered severe panic attacks if a door slammed or some other sudden sound rang out.

With the memories of the horrors of war foremost in most people's minds, throughout our childhood we were all taught that because of the great sacrifices endured at war we were blessed to live in freedom and could live in peace.

We were known as the lucky generation.

At school we were taught how the United Nations was formed and how the Human Rights Declarations were signed by all the Nations of the free world, so that democratically elected Governments of those countries would protect all people with International Human Rights laws to the standards laid down in the Universal Declaration of Human Rights and subsequent Declarations agreed and signed since.

Clearly the Government in the UK have abdicated their obligations to provide the fundamental right to the rule of law to Alan Bates and the hundreds of other Sub Post Masters who have been destroyed (some committed suicide) and made to be scapegoats to hide the fact that the Post Office's major investment in the Horizon computer system at huge public cost was defective.

They vigorously defended the suppliers of the Horizon computer system that had been developed by UK software company International Computers Limited (ICL) which was subsequently sold to the Japanese IT giant Fujitsu. The heartless "Post Office brand first" culture of the executives culminated in the Sub Postmasters being accused of theft to hide the IT systems short comings even though they were totally innocent of any wrongdoing.

The management's reaction was probably to cover the back sides of the executives who had made the purchase in the first place.

They didn't want to admit that they had spent massive amounts of Tax Payers money on a faulty computer program for which they probably had been paid bonuses for stitching the deal together at the outset.

The anomaly is that rather than uphold the high standards expected by the declarations signed by the Governments of the British Commonwealth, the politicians have actually created a big sponge for the Government and Corporate's hierarchy to hide behind, leaving the community with no effective protection from big business and/or official brutality.

The emotions that were stirred up in me watching Mr Bates vs the Post Office program gave me that gnawing feeling in the pit of my stomach that quickly developed into the renewed inspiration to get our boxes of evidence that had been stored all over the place and carry on fighting to demand for deliverance of the basic rights that have been promised to us, just like Alan Bates has done.

Or if nothing else, to ensure that New Zealanders are made aware of the fact that our Government has been misleading the people to believe that we have Human Rights that in reality the State is unable to uphold due to an unworkable legislature that is subservient to the big player's power of money.

In our case it was as early as 1995 that we had discovered that our bank, the Bank of New Zealand (BNZ) was stealing money from our business accounts by secretly loading interest charges amounting to a significant amount of money. The amounts of money involved, as we later discovered, had actually engineered a situation that the bank claimed that we were in default of our loan payments, when in fact they had taken far more money than the amount of the claimed default.

They claimed to have contractual rights to penalise us based on that false default.

The bank continued charging penalties though and refused to return the overcharges for years while they continued to screw the businesses accounts down to an impossible situation.

The power a bank gets over you if a mortgage payment default occurs is something most mortgage holders are unaware of and I have seen many people suffer the draconian actions that can follow, much to their confusion and disbelief.

The threats and the blackmail can be so overpowering that some people panic and commit suicide for the fear of failure from the thinly disguised threats they receive.

Others become depressed and go into their shell, take drugs and alcohol and wishing it would all go away, but their situation progressively worsens and often ill health develops.

Just like Mr Bates we had complained to our personal bank manager thinking the charges were simply a mistake and like

Alan Bates a focus was directed at the bank's computer program, but rather than make corrections the bank became aggressive towards us and to our bewilderment it was very soon that we were led into a dispute that ultimately escalated into a total financial collapse.

We offered to show the Bank how we had discovered the overcharges, but that offer was met with distain and a further tightening of the noose.

The executive based in head office in Wellington who eventually had been tasked to recreate the statements to identify the total amount of the overcharges had an enormous struggle and actually contacted us from time to time asking for us to explain the method we used to establish the correct figures.

We concluded that this man (the second longest staff member of the bank) had no idea about the practices the branches were using to boost their monthly figures, but in the process of correcting the figures, unless the precise figures used in a particular Branch were known it would be of very little help anyway.

We kept putting up quantified and qualified documents seeking recognition that it was the banks dodgy practice of overcharging interest on our business accounts and the management's bad attitude that was the core issue that needed to be addressed, but good sense seemed to be a foreign concept to the banks executives, and the rot set in.

The inhuman corporate culture took over.

Although watching the ITV story was very sombre, like the scene when Alan Bates was putting his boxes of evidence into the attic, made me realized why I was struggling to "just get over it and move on" as so many people had been telling me to do for years. I could see that Alan Bates had felt the same feeling of disbelief that I have from the burden of injustice on you knowing that you have been wrongly punished and/or discredited. As I'm sure Alan Bates would agree that as time passes the feelings of injustice grow to become a very hard load to carry and it is near on impossible not to take on board some of the baggage of other victims when you meet them.

This feeling can be best described as being just like the time I got the strap in front of the class when we were all having a singing lesson one day at school. I liked music and singing along as we did this a lot at home around the piano because our farther was a very good player and played the piano a lot. No TV in those days.

On the day at the Apiti School during the radio broadcast singing class, I was standing by my desk and smiling as I was singing. For some unknown reason the teacher must have thought I was being a smart ass, so he hauled me out to the front of the class and strapped me, while the radio program kept on singing away. I will always remember that injustice because I had done nothing wrong, so it wasn't fair. I had the strap other times when I must have done something wrong, but I can't remember those times, but obviously the feeling of the injustice of being punished unfairly never seems to leave our memory.

In the ITV story, the moment Alan Bates gave an odd but knowing expression to his wife Suzanne when she had indicated that she was secretly hoping he might be going to leave it all behind him, the message of his facial expression went right through me; obviously Suzanne had seen his look in the same way as I had by her knowing smile. (Good acting skills)

Mr Bates give up – No way – He knows he is right.

At that moment I started thinking about the unfinished business of our fight and got that gut feeling that the bastards had got away with it, (the baddies got off scot free as Alan Bates would say) so at that moment I decided to revisit the mountain of boxes and cabinets of documents that detailed the injustice that we had been fighting for over 24 years, just like Alan Bates and the many other falsely accused sub Postmasters did.

Our fight has been running over the same period that the Bates and the hundreds of other victims he had bought together who have also been fighting for common justice seemingly for ever. Around the same time of the Post Office expose', both the drama and the documentary were being screened internationally, and In New Zealand Jack Tame (NZ Journalist of the Year 2024) interviewed the real Alan Bates on his Saturday morning show on Radio ZB Talkback. During the interview Mr Bates told Jack that he believes the UK Government has a duty to deliver the justice and compensation owed to the Sub Postmasters he represents, because like me he knows they have failed to uphold the basic level of human rights that promises all people protection under the rule of law for illegal acts committed against them.

To deliberately prosecute a person based on lies to cover up for a corporate deal gone wrong is definitely an illegal act.

Suddenly I could see the parallel that the New Zealand Government had exactly the same obligation to the citizens of New Zealand under the same declarations of human rights that apply in the UK.

That of course is exactly what the New Zealand Chief Human Rights Commissioner had told Hon Peter Dunne, 20 years ago.

The realization that the pain I have been burdened with over recent years is that of being defeated and I was giving in to platitudes and was giving up. That hurts!

Mr Bates Vs the Post Office has rekindled the only motivation that has been keeping me going for 24 years. Depression subsides when I am actively working on finding ways to be heard, probably because as Winston Peters said when the same "bully boys" were discrediting his efforts during the Wine Box expose' "if you are right you fight" so now I must remember the rule, to beat the depression, we are right, so we must fight.

The UK Post Office scandal has been described by many as the greatest miscarriage of justice in British legal history.

So what about New Zealand?

During the same period that the events recorded in this book, the:

United Nations - General Assembly - Human Rights Council – Working Group on the Universal Periodic Review of New Zealand's Human Rights standards made the following judgment and recommendations:

"At New Zealand's last Periodic Report in 2002 the Committee again urged the New Zealand Government to take appropriate steps to ensure remedies are available in accordance with Article 2 of the International Covenant on Civil and Political Rights (ICCPR)".

"The Development of Judicial remedies

…. Court of Appeal held that effective and appropriate Remedies are available for breach of the Bill of Right Act.

We would fail in our duty if we did not give an effective remedy to a person whose legislative affirmed rights have been infringed.

Remedies under the International Treaties

Unlike the Bill of Rights Act, International Human Rights Treaties provide for express remedies. EG:

1. The International Covenant on Civil and Political Rights ("ICCPR")

Article 2 (3) of the ICCPR requires New Zealand to:

(a) Ensure any person who's covenant rights are violated has an effective remedy;
(b) Develop the possibilities of judicial remedy; and
(c) Ensure any person claiming a remedy has his or her right enforced by competent authorities".

"Principle subjects of concern and recommendations

The State party (New Zealand) should enact legislation giving full effort to all Covenant rights and provide victims with access to effective remedies with the domestic legal system. It should also strengthen the current mechanisms to ensure compatibility of domestic law with the Covenant".

(In 2000 the BNZ had manipulated the "domestic legal system" process to bankrupt us and the Government stood by and did nothing)

"Remedies compensation and rehabilitation.

Individuals who consider that any of their rights under BORA have been infringed can bring an action against the Government. A number of remedies are available, including the ability to award damages or compensation and to exclude any evidence obtained in breach of a right guaranteed by the BORA. New Zealand Courts can also order a stay in proceedings where there has been a delay of such a length that it constitutes a breach of Section 25 (b) of the BORA".

The New Zealand Bill of Rights Act (BORA) is affirmed to the Universal Declaration of Human Rights: This declaration was proclaimed by the United Nations on 10th December 1948. The State of New Zealand is a signatory to this internationally recognised declaration as the founding document of the free world.

Having been knocking on the doors of every level of Government during the period covered in the United Nations Human Rights Council Periodic Report it can be concluded that the New Zealand Government totally ignored the United Nations Human Rights Council directive to provide all people with effective remedies for violations of their rights.

…Universal Declaration of Human Rights

Article 8:

Everyone has the right to an effective remedy by the competent national tribunals for acts violating the fundamental rights granted him by the constitution or by law.

During the search for a just hearing we have held numerous communications and meetings with many offices of authority over compliance enforcement, who invariably interpret that human rights declared, such as the above, have some other obscure meaning rather than to be delivered to people like us. (All People) When we keep getting told you can't fight a bank, are we being told that a bank can break the law, but you can't?

For example individual officers of the Human Rights Commission say that they are only there to help people who have been discriminated against, (do they mean Human Rights weren't declared to uphold justice?), therefore the emphasis of their work is directed at issues that involve isms like sexism, racism, ageism, sexual orientation and God help us the right to identify as whatever we wish to. If a kid wants to identify as a cat, why shouldn't they?

Well bugger me.

These isms are not the Human Rights and freedoms that our forefathers fought, spilled blood and died for. The fundamental purpose of International Human Rights law is that all rights are promised to all people without any discrimination.

Chapter 2

Mr Bates Vs Post Office ITV expose'

Having watched the ITV drama and the documentary footage the Eatwell's have identified so many of the tactics that the British Post Office had imposed on the Sub Postmasters that were all too familiar to them and many other victims of the Bank of New Zealand's bad practices and the gross injustice that followed.

Toby Jones as Alan Bates in the ITV drama played out in the story, and subsequently as the real Alan Bates said at the official inquiry into the UK Horizon scandal that he and his wife Suzanne had invested in the shop with a Post Office agency in Craig-Don, Wales in 1998. He explained how the negotiations with the Post Office had been quite convivial with the Post Office sales executives glowingly explaining how they would be partners with Alan Bates and his wife Suzanne, so they happily poured all their savings into the business expecting a prosperous future.

Why shouldn't they have?

While in little Old New Zealand the Bank of New Zealand personal bank managers were flat out wooing new customers in their aggressive drive for increased market share by telling their prospective new customers they would be their partners too. But sadly, as Alan Bates told the UK inquiry the partnership very soon after they had committed to the contract with the Post Office the partnership became one sided with Post Office hierarchy becoming quite demanding, in fact by 2003 the Bates had been sacked, or should we say divorced. While in New Zealand the Bank of New Zealand partnership with people like the Eatwell's and their companies the bank only waited a few months to start stealing their money by over loading interest charges. Just like Alan and Suzanne Bates the Eatwell family got the sack (divorced) in 1998 when the Bank ignored the High Court process ("domestic legal system") and put the Eatwell business's into receivership.

In the book "You can Bank on it" the partnership arrangement was described as:

"No sooner had I said "I do" or was it "I will" and the dirty little bankers were shafting me.

Seemingly no further consents were required either, because I was taken however and when- ever the gluttonous banker desired.

Had I mistaken those grins of lust as smiles of agreement"?

From the book "You can Bank on it" the partnership with the BNZ was very one sided.

It has been well noted that individual Sub Post Masters were isolated by the Post Office executives telling them they were the only ones complaining about the IT problems. This was the same kind of tactic the Bankers used when they told customers they had in the thumb screws that they were the only customers of the bank complaining about bank practices, or at best they would say their account was the worst case they had in their branch.

The age old tactic of divide and rule by villainising the person who complained.

The UK Post Office insisted that the individual Sub Post Masters must pay the ever increasing short falls being coughed out by the computer program, stating they were contracted to do so, even though the Sub Post Masters protested that they had not stolen any money and insisted there was a mistake in the computer system, whereas, by comparison in New Zealand the Bank of New Zealand charged excess penalties and froze the bank accounts of complaining customers and took steps to bankrupt them, also sighting contractual rights to do so.

They quickly forgot to consider their own contractual obligations in the loan process though and the statutory law keepers stood by and did nothing.

Throughout the whole process in the UK, the Post Office had obfuscated the truth at every attempt that was made to investigate the complaints, but in New Zealand the bank totally distorted the truth or at best they just ignored many levels of Parliament, Government, Banking Ombudsman, and the High Court.

In a letter to the Prime Minister Helen Clark, the chairman of the Board of the BNZ said that the BCAC pleadings to him and his bank contained nothing but "Hyperbole and an absence of facts", which was a total distortion of the facts that had been presented to him.

It is thought that it was this influence that the Government had adopted when they blocked every effort that was made for the Eatwell's case to be properly heard.

In the UK the Post Office has the right to run its own prosecutions.

Thus the Post Office prosecuted Sub Post Masters and had them thrown in jail, while in New Zealand the Bank manipulated the law Courts to impose receiverships and bankruptcy on complaining customers.

In the same way that disgraced Sub Post Masters who had been crushed by the failure of their business in this way is mirrored by many of the victims of the BNZ who also found they were outcast by the community they lived in and even people who they thought were friends and some family members would shun them. They couldn't borrow money, get a mortgage or rebuild a business for many years. It was even hard to open a bank account and when they did, the account would be flagged so they could only withdraw a minimal amount of money at one time. At times this meant that enough food could not be purchased on a given day. Not easy if you live out of town.

The bankers would make accusations to the police that customers may become violent at a particular event or time, so the police would send Officers to attend auctions of plant and machinery and other means of hocking off peoples possessions under forced sales of their hard earned assets.

The ongoing damage to the lives of broken Sub Post Masters who had been outcast in their communities, suffered deep depression causing pressure on marriages leading to relationship breakdowns, in desperation some had involved family to support them financially, some contracted stress invoked Cancer and other health issues. The draconian measures imposed on them were too much for some individual Sub Postmasters who ended it all and committed suicide.

Sadly the same effects of the persecution Bank of New Zealand customers have suffered also caused the same disastrous human destruction of many good people in New Zealand.

Since the ITV expose' of the story Mr Bates Vs the Post Office there have been various statements made stating that the treatment of the Sub Post Masters by the Post Office management and lawyers etc has to be the worst corruption of justice ever seen in the UK.

By comparison it is a travesty to say that hundreds of victims of the draconian practices of the Bank of New Zealand and their henchmen have suffered just as badly as the Sub Post

Masters have from the comparable institutional injustice that has been exposed in the UK.

Unbeknown to the Eatwell's there had been a TV expose' of the National Australia Bank owned National Irish Bank screened in Ireland in March 1998 , exposing information that the Irish bank had been caught stealing customers money by the same overloading interest and fees practice they had discovered at the National Australia owned, Bank of New Zealand. In Ireland the evidence of malpractice was first shown in public by RTE (Irish national TV) led the Irish Government to invoke a High Court investigation, during which the Irish High Court found that the bank had been stealing money off its customers and dodging tax by scandalous methods using customer's funds to do so since the 1980's, which coincided with the National Irish Bank being taken over by the National Australia Bank.

Unfortunately for the Eatwell's and other effected customers of the BNZ, it wasn't until the Irish High Court report was published in 2004 that the illicit practices involved were exposed to them. The detail of the Irish report showing the actual method the bankers had used to load interest charges on selected accounts demonstrated how the overcharges showing on BNZ monthly statement figures had been manoeuvred in such a way as to be extremely difficult to be identified by a customer.

The BCAC went through a lot of peoples bank statements for them and found a lot of overcharges in them; in fact there were very few that didn't have loaded charges, particularly when the loan documents were referenced in the calculations. Mr Eatwell often said that some of the statements checked had the person's accountant's signature at the bottom of each page to show that the statement had been checked by them. However the overcharged interest and fees were so well hidden that the accountants hadn't picked up on the illegal overcharges that had been pilfered off their client.

It is also interesting to note that the Mr Bates Vs the Post Office scandal was initially recognised by Rebecca Thomson a Journalist from the Computer Weekly in the UK who investigated and published her story of the Post Office malpractice in the weekly magazine in 2009.

It raises the question as to why it takes public exposure before the official offices of Government do their job to uphold the conditions of statute, while it always seems to take some media attention before the failure of the Corporates to honour their statutory obligations to the people is identified.

Most public offices employ media people these days to put out sanitised press releases to fudge what is really going on in a particular department and make the processes look good or at least look better to the public. Unfortunately these people are also wheeled out when the media comes sniffing about and are very well versed in the spin doctors codes with all the fob offs like privacy issues and other feeble excuses to keep the truth from being told.

It beggars believe that in New Zealand TVNZ 60 Minutes screened the story about the Eatwell battle with the BNZ, making it very clear that the foundation of the problems was the interest overcharging and the banks refusal to correct the effects of the practice. Vickie Eatwell said that they had been "stolen from" by the bank at a very sensitive moment of the documentary.

The mind boggles to think that the 60 Minutes producers didn't know about the RTE expose' in Ireland. The Irish Journalists George Lee and Charlie Bird were awarded the Journalist of the year in 1998 with some fan fair for their efforts.

There is no doubt that Mike Valentine and Sallie Stone of the 60 Minutes TV crew would have loved to receive comparable accolades for their exposing the fact that a New Zealand Bank had stolen from its customers, just as it had been exposed in Ireland by RTE uncovering evidence of the same theft of customers money by the Irish bank.

Maybe they did know, but kept their heads down knowing how vindictive the banking industry can be in New Zealand, or possibly not, but it is hard to imagine how a high profile international current affairs team like 60 Minutes were not connected with their peers overseas when they were making such an expose' that involved an international corporate bank.

In 2024 an official judicial inquiry was commissioned after the revelations of the ITV expose' in the UK, at last, but this in itself is just prolonging the travesty to the victims and could drag on for months and/or years.

Alan Bates has said he is also very aware of that risk, because they have tried to short change him on two offers of compensation already, offering one sixth and one third of his carefully quantified claim.

Corporate and Government executives just can't help themselves, so beware.

However, at least there is an official investigation taking place at last in the UK, whereas in New Zealand doors of authority are firmly shut and the big corporates just keep on getting away with their crimes and bleeding the economy by taking excessive profits from their unprotected customers.

With these facts now known it is very hard to accept that the system is still in stalled mode particularly when we see and hear the tenacity Alan Bates has demonstrated, therefore while we know that the denial of justice for the victims of the crimes committed by the Bank of New Zealand have not been prosecuted and the individual victims have never been vindicated, those individuals that hold the obligations of being elected to represent the State in both countries are duty bound to uphold the promises of our democratic society, and it is they who must be held to account.

It is wrong to proclaim that natural justice exists in New Zealand, when serious matters of dispute involving large corporates such as a bank can be ignored, while the officers of the New Zealand Government continue to hide behind the delusion that we live in a fair and just society. It is only a guise that suits the highly paid authorities, because the State is being administered by offices occupied by toothless tigers that have no authority to enforce the States fundamental obligations to uphold common law, therefore the international obligations of State are being denied.

In reality the authorities at every level have failed dismally to uphold the fundamental Human Rights obligations as recorded in the Bill of Rights Act and the international declarations it is affirmed to, which in effect leaves customers in a dispute with their bank totally unprotected from the oppression of over powered banks in New Zealand.

Lest we forget the foundation of those sacred declarations, won with the lives and spilled blood that was sacrificed to invoke them.

Chapter 3

Media exposed foul play

In reply to an email congratulating one of the journalists who first exposed the UK Post Office scandal his reply said, *"it's so frustrating watching those with power and influence trample on people unchallenged …….. Credit should go to the victims and campaigners who fought for justice. It feels surreal what the Post Office tried to do, and they almost got away with it."*

All too often the thuggery of the big players is actually protected by the executives of Government Offices of Authority and other law enforcement agencies who abdicate their mandated obligations, so in reality illegal corporate practice is only exposed by the persistence of some very good journalists within the Fourth Estate.

Mostly when the media starts investigating big business corruption the offices of authority mandated to enforce compliance to the law actually obstruct the journalists by closing ranks and hiding information and/ or fudging it.

We can only shudder to think how much big business corruption is covered up and they do just get away with it, because they hide the truth by shutting the media out. Mainly by the use of bully boy tactics of threats to sue that are relayed by high flying lawyers who use the Courts as a weapon to defeat free speech. Or else they will tell a media outlet that if you don't run that story we will give you a heap of advertising, or on the flip side of that if they already have advertising with the firm they threaten to pull it off them if they print/play/ air the story in question.

There were many examples of the UK Post Office's executives determination to hide the truth with examples of the cover-up's by executive staff that are being exposed by the current UK inquiry, where several individual witnesses have been found out in several ways during the hearings.

One witness, Barrister Simon Clarke, who had worked for the Post Office, described his shock at learning a Post Office witness had misled the Court in the 2013 inquiry, saying that the Post Office security chief had suggested that the minutes of meetings be shredded.

Several of the Lawyers and other witnesses being questioned at the current UK inquiry are fobbing off questions by claiming memory loss, but the Counsel Jason Beer KC and other Counsel invariably catch them out with electronic evidence of actions made on the individual's computer that provide evidence of the time that specific actions had occurred. Even with this level of proof some of those being questioned still deny any knowledge of their involvement in pushing the buttons as it is recorded on their computer's hard drive.

The "not me syndrome" is very obvious in some of the witnesses on the stand.

"No not me Guv" as Lord James Arbuthnot would say.

In New Zealand the TVNZ 60 Minutes documentary was screened on 15th November 1998 that exposed malpractices enforced on the Eatwell Companies from Franz Josef by the Bank of New Zealand.

The documentary was entitled "A Pack of Bankers" and was produced by Sallie Stone and fronted by Mike Valentine who recreated the story of a dispute with a bank that had ended in total ruin for the Eatwell family. Details of how they had discovered that the Bank was secretly taking excessive interest payments and how the complaints they had made to the bank about it had deteriorated into a hopeless situation, was featured.

Following excerpts are copied from the TVNZ 60 Minutes run sheet:

60 Minutes: A pack of Bankers

15th November 1998

Gray and Vickie Eatwell are Westcoast farmers who have lost their farm property to the BNZ. This is after the BNZ had encouraged their borrowing, taken over $1 million in interest, miscalculated their interest rates and refused to refund the entire amount owed. Their foreclosure deal with the Eatwells was dependent on the Eatwells dropping their claim against the BNZ to the Banking Ombudsman.

Shot List:

01: 04: 1 MS: Gray Eatwell, West coast farmer, who has BNZ foreclose on his farm.

01: 04:20: I/V: Vickie Eatwell, with Gray Eatwell, reply, they don't care about the lives they are effecting, we have had meetings with these people (BNZ), they are expressionless, we might as well talk to the window.

01:05:10 I/V: Gray Eatwell re I know I've made mistakes; we wouldn't be faced with this dilemma if we had not been involved with the Bank of New Zealand (BNZ)

01: 05:42 I/V Owen Jennings, ACT list MP, re there's claims and counter claims of course.

01:05:54 I/V: Owen Jennings re Lack of professionalism by the bank from early on has been surprising and has contributed toward difficulties faced by Eatwell family and the bank.

01: 06: 12: I/V Vickie Eatwell re being ripped off, yes, they've overcharged interest, and they've agreed, theft, ripped off, financially and emotionally.

01:06:34: GV: Gray Eatwell and his daughter checking daily interest rates against bank charges on their overdraft accounts.

01:06:58 I/V: Gray Eatwell discovering BNZ had overcharged on overdraft accounts, 3 months after we (went with BNZ) they started charging us, in 9th month they overcharged $1,200 for the month, no explanation, its taken three and a half years to get any of it back.

01:07:44 I/V: Gray Eatwell re BNZ not acknowledging outstanding amount from BNZ overcharges and long term loan, as far as we can see the interest rate that has been used is sometimes an excess rate, or a figure plucked out of the air, the rate is inconsistent.

01:08:02 I/V: Owen Jennings re bank have a lot of explaining to do its 1000's of dollars at a time when their customer was under pressure anyway, we did once believe that banks never made mistakes.

01:08:50 I/V: David Russell re weather its legally required or not is immaterial, bank has moral obligation to let them know what went wrong with the system, maybe there are any number of consumers that are affected by it too.

01:10:41 I/V : Gray Eatwell: re bank was encouraging us to borrow money, we turned away as much money from the bank as we ever uplifted.

01:10:59 I/V: Gray Eatwell re (BNZ) never honoured agreements we had and support through highs and lows of our business, when the climate changed it was withdrawn, the interest rates increased, the bank refused to refund those overcharges.

01: 13:19 I/V: Vickie Eatwell re disgraceful, they brow beat you, they're bullies.

01:13:42 I/V: David Russell re threats and blackmail that the bank will reach settlement provided Eatwells withdraw complaint to Banking Ombudsman, I find that totally unacceptable.

01:14:29 I/V: Gray Eatwell re I've asked everyone from the girl on the desk to the board of directors to sit down and talk to me.

In one scene Vickie had told the reporter that they had been ripped off and stolen from by the bank, while Gray sitting on a bale of hay in the barn with Mike Valentine admitted to having demons that had made him consider ending it all like others had.

David Russell was a well-recognised consumer watch dog and was a member of the Banking Ombudsman Commission at the time, while Owen Jennings had been the president of Federated Farmers for some time prior to being elected to Parliament on the Act party list.

The CEO of the BNZ Mike Pratt had initially agreed to be interviewed by 60 minutes, but after the crew had flown to Wellington the CEO refused the interview. The bank sent a written statement saying they had done everything they could and that was screened at the end of the program.

Yeah Right! Everything, but the truth Mike.

The word was out because the Australian banker's cartel jumped into action; within a couple of days before the documentary was to go to air, another Australian Bank, Westpac contacted 60 Minutes and threatened to take away all of their advertising on TVNZ if the 60 minutes program went to air.

TVNZ 60 Minutes stood firm on the obligations of the Fourth Estate and broadcast the program as scheduled. The documentary was also shown throughout Australia soon after.

The question that should be asked is what was the banking Industry trying to hide when Westpac made the threats to TVNZ?

Maybe it was just that they don't want prying eyes to see what sneaky practices they are up to when creating the massive profits they suck out of their blind Kiwi customer's accounts.

The other burning question would have to be, what the BNZ hierarchy said to the Westpac executives, (who should have had no idea what the program was about) that would make them expose themselves to an internationally recognised documentary maker like 60 Minutes. For a major competitor bank to firstly be asked to, and secondly to allow themselves to be directly involved in making threats to silence the media, smells very much like there must be a cartel operating within the Australian owned banks in New Zealand.

If not, why would such threats have been made?

Hearing the Governor of the Reserve Bank this week (May 21st 2024) makes you wonder when he identifies the impact the Australian owned banks are having on preventing effective competition in the banking services in New Zealand.

With the benefit of time and the development of the internet we now know the National Australia Bank who own the Bank of New Zealand also owned the National Irish Bank in Ireland, and the two banks owned by them had directors on both boards of directors and we know that one such director was also the CEO of the Nab in Australia.

We now know that at the same time the Eatwells had identified overcharging on their BNZ accounts the bank's Governors had full knowledge that the same practice was happening in Ireland and that the Irish High Court was investigating the malpractices involved.

Journalists from Radio Telefis Eireann (RTE) Television got wind of the Irish bank carrying out overcharging and tax dodging practices, but when the bank learned of the snooping that the Journalists George Lee and Charlie Bird were doing they took out a gagging order by the way of an injunction issued by the Court.

It took some time to shake off the injunction, but a victory for the truth was pursued by Mr Lee and Mr Bird and their management and eventually they were able to go to air in March 1998 and expose the rotten tactics of the NIB. The RTE expose' prompted the Irish Government to invoke the High Court investigation that culminated in the Director of Corporate Enforcement Paul Appleby publishing his report on 31st July 2004, 6 years later.

It took another 10 years to get prosecutions to stick on some of the Directors and managers involved.

Given that the depth of the corruption that has been uncovered as a result of the exposures that have only been investigated after many years by the tenacity of some good journalists of the Fourth Estate, we must contemplate how much more corruption is being protected by the corporate culture to overpower anyone who tries to question their illegal practices. Or maybe as the Westpac Bank tried to do, they will apply their power of money and/or the influence over the Government and its agencies over whom the absolute power of money also dictates.

Credit must go to those individuals who challenge the lies, threats, blackmail and bribery, whether they do it as their job or as a victim of the corruption (or perish the thought a public servant upholding their mandate), but if justice is to prevail the truth must be delivered for the sake of the future stability for the people of the free world.

The free market is a long way from being free; the fact is the more the market forces are leaned on to dictate controls over industry the more corruption "gets off scot free".

It was only when Rebecca Thomson and Karl Flinders from the Computer Weekly opened up the UK Post Office scandal, and George Lee and Charlie Bird of the RTE opened up the NIB scandal in Ireland and Mike Valentine and Sallie Stone of TVNZ 60 minutes exposed the BNZ's malpractice to the public that things happened. Slowly, very slowly.

Well not so much in New Zealand, unfortunately.

There was one situation when Tim Hunter a well-recognised business reporter of the Sunday Star Times (at the time) had written a comprehensive story about the Eatwell/BNZ case based on substantial documented evidence supplied to him. The article was scheduled to be published in the Sunday Star Times the following week-end, but the BNZ intervened and bribed the Editors of the Sunday Star Times by offering to buy a full centre page advertisement worth a lot of money to the paper, but only if they pulled the Eatwell story of course. That story was never published as it had been written, but a seriously misleading statement supplied by the bank was printed instead and sadly the "Fourth Estate" had been defeated, that time.

The editor of the Sunday Star Times would have been quite happy because there was a double centre page flamboyant advertisement about how wonderful the BNZ is, in the Sunday paper that week-end.

What a coincidence.

Many Journalists wrote articles about the Eatwell vs BNZ saga in New Zealand, but most were worn down by the pressure applied from the top. Ian Wishart wrote about the BNZ (including the Eatwell story) in the first edition of the book "Daylight Robbery" and Gray Eatwell wrote the book "You can Bank on it" first published in 2001, but the BNZ still got off "scot free" simply because they have the Government in their pocket, which continues to stand by and allow them to keep, "trampling on people and go unchallenged".

As Karl Flinders said in his email, credit must go to Alan Bates for showing enormous courage and determination to hold on to his absolute belief that justice must be done, for over 23 years, because it was his lead that gave the inspiration to pursue justice in New Zealand so that if nothing else the BNZ scandal that has also taken 25 years of twists, turns, blind alleys and abdications of statutory duty, must also be told.

Chapter 4

National Australia Bank owned

National Irish Bank

May 1997: A businessman from Cork in Ireland wrote to Don Argus chief executive of National Irish Bank's (NIBs) parent bank the National Australia Bank (Nab), Don Argus had been a director on the board of directors of the National Irish Bank (NIB) since 1990.

In his letter the Cork businessman told the Australian CEO about his problems with the bank, saying that the Clerical Medical Insurance (CIM) scheme was a scandal. He explained how the NIB bank manager had arranged a meeting with him at his work place to discuss opportunities for him to invest money that he had on deposit at the bank. The bank manager duly arrived, as arranged, with a NIB investment sales person and one of the banks Dublin-based investment managers in tow. They had bought a range of charts and reports and delivered a lengthy and quite glossy presentation of the scheme. He said how they had pushed him very hard to sign up for the deal, but he had baulked when they had mentioned the amounts of money that would be charged by the bank.

He couldn't understand why it was so expensive and why they had failed to offer any interest advantage this complicated scheme had over the savings accounts he already had at the bank.

Quite some time after this meeting, a client of the Cork businessman had gone into liquidation owing his business over 600,000 Pounds. However without any warning or explanation the bank froze all of the businessman's bank accounts including the savings accounts (some of which were in bogus names) and with no access to any money his business quickly ground to a stand-still.

He was a man of substantial means, but with the strangle hold his bank had over him he was unable to operate his business and was essentially shut down.

Obviously this surprise action caused this customer to seek an explanation from NIB, about their actions, but they blithely dismissed his queries, so eventually the situation turned into a dispute that got very tense and bitter, particularly as he could see he was being pushed into bankruptcy. So with a fear of imminent ruin he decided in desperation to write the letter to Don Argus to explain the reason for him making the complaints to NIB in the first place. He made a point of expressing his disgust at the pressure the bank had put on him when trying to convince him to be roped into the dodgy offshore scheme. He even offered to fly the Nab CEO over to Ireland, and to put him up in a hotel to give him the opportunity to explain what was going on at his Irish bank.

(Obviously he was thinking that Don Argus didn't know.)

There was no reply to the letter and No Don on the plane, but worse still nothing was done to resolve the dispute following the letter either. Therefore, as he was labouring under the huge stress this had caused him, the business man reluctantly decided to speak to the Radio Telefis Eireann (RTE) (Irish TV) journalists George Lee and Charlie Bird with a desperate hope that a resolution would be found to save his business from total collapse and prevent him being forced into bankruptcy. He was a fair minded man, so in his mind he thought good sense would surely follow and justice would prevail.

Why would it not?

15th January 1998: Following secret accusations of foul play at the bank they had received, the RTE Journalists began their investigation in earnest.

30th January 1998: (Exerts taken from The Irish High Court condensed report):

- Judge Patrick Smith granted an injunction of the National Irish Bank Limited v Radio Telefis Eireann

(RTE) that was applied for by the bank in an effort to scuttle the Journalists investigation. But RTE was determined that the Fourth Estate would not be silenced and worked on a way they could safely proceed to air. This was achieved when the injunction was lifted by the Court and the revelations became public knowledge that rocked Ireland.

- **January 1998:** An unidentified bank employee approaches RTÉ with allegations that National Irish Bank (NIB) had been taking money from customer accounts for no legitimate reason, systematically overcharged interest and fees and operated an offshore investment scheme that enabled some of its customers to evade tax. NIB obtains a temporary injunction in the High Court to prevent RTÉ broadcasting the story, but loses its case in the Supreme Court

- **Mid 1998:** Following an internal investigation by Arthur Anderson accountants, NIB agrees to return €166,500 plus interest to customers who had been overcharged.

- **March 1998:** Minister for Enterprise, Trade and Employment Ms Harney appoints two High Court inspectors - Mr Justice Blayney, a former Supreme Court judge, and accountant Mr Tom Grace - to investigate activities at NIB since 1988. They are given wide powers to interview witnesses and obtain bank documents.

23rd March 1998: The Irish Government had gone into an emergency cabinet session following the RTE revelations of the serious malpractices of the National Irish Bank. The fourth largest bank in Ireland had been caught stealing money from customer's accounts impacting on the people's confidence in the entire Irish banking system that had been seriously undermined by malpractice at the NIB.

RTE TV had exposed the wrongdoings of NIB including the practice of overcharging customers interest and the scandalous tax dodges the Cork business man had explained, while stating that the bank was only selling the dodgy schemes to a select group of customers.

March 26th 1998: Ross Pinney the CEO of the National Australia Bank in Europe, who was also a director on the board of the Bank of New Zealand at the time, was summoned to a crisis meeting at the Central Bank of Ireland. In urgency the Central Bank had insisted that Don Argus appealed to the bank's depositors to prevent a run on the bank and to avoid a potential financial calamity.

(There was a Don on the plane from Australia this time!)

October 1998: The RTE journalists George Lee and Charlie Bird were awarded Journalists of the year for their gallant efforts to expose this blatant scandal. They also co- wrote a book to explain how they had uncovered the banks crimes under the title "Breaking the Bank" published in 1998. NB: The 60 minutes documentary about the Eatwell case with the bank of New Zealand was filmed in October 1998 and screened on 15th November that year. (Vickie's birthday 24th October featured in the TV program).

Unfortunately this drama played out pre-google and with minimal internet available at the time, so in New Zealand we had no knowledge of the situation in Ireland and so the facts only emerged in New Zealand when the Irish Director of Corporate Enforcement Paul Appleby's High Court report was published in 2004, however with the knowledge we now have from the report it is hard not to conclude that the illegal practices that had been exposed at the BNZ during the same period most likely were carried out with the same processes that the Irish High Court report found had been the practice at the Irish bank.

The Irish bank staff had been schooled by the new Australian owners just like the BNZ staff had been trained after Nab had bought the New Zealand bank.

28th October 1998: On behalf of Eatwell Livestock Limited a letter marked urgent was sent by the Bank Customer Action Collective to Mr Don Argus CEO of National Australia Bank also intending to advise him of what his New Zealand bank was doing, by saying, *"We would like to draw your attention to an extremely serious issue that we feel as the owners of the Bank of New Zealand you should be made aware of, along with our appeal for assistance as it has not been available from within the New Zealand system."* Amongst other anomalies of the Bank of New Zealand the matter of *"serious interest overcharging"* of the customer was made clear to him. The Bank Customer Action Collective (BCAC) was not aware that Don Argus was on the board of directors of the BNZ and was oblivious of the Irish scandal at that time.

Very much like the Irish case the Eatwell's had tried for several years to have the overcharges they had discovered addressed in house without any satisfactory action by the Bank and just like the Cork businessman their complaints quickly developed into a dispute with the bank.

The absolute confusion of trying to understand why the BNZ managers were acting so aggressively is exposed in the book "You can Bank on it". Written by Gray Eatwell, published December 2001.

Forward:

"This book is about a crucial part of our society-the Banking industry. In particular the Bank of New Zealand. It is a summary of the treatment that I received from the BNZ bankers. This bad experience has exposed a culture to me that runs rough shod over codes of common decency and ethics that New Zealanders should be entitled to expect from their bankers".

Following the letter to Don Argus there was no reply and nothing was done to resolve the dispute with the BNZ, but 10 days later receivers arrived at the Eatwell's large farm property at Franz Josef and took full control of the business from the family.

Obviously the all-powerful Don Argus had chosen to ignore the fact that his bank had broken the law by the overcharging practice and that there was a High Court claim lodged against the BNZ. Obviously he decided that the best approach was to shut the problem down aggressively with the same arrogance that his Irish bank was being deliberately uncooperative with the Irish High Court inspectors at that date.

They would most probably have been buying time to clean up the documents before they let the inspector's sticky beaks into them. A bit like the UK Post Office executive who wanted to shred meeting minutes, so they couldn't be seen by investigators.

While the banker's decision to crush the Eatwells was no different to the actions the Post Office had applied to the Sub Postmasters in the UK during the same period of time.

If the bankers and the UK Post Office had any corporate integrity at all it is hard to reconcile how the executives of those organisations could have the actions they had implemented on their conscience, for example how could Don Argus have found any solace for his choice to ignore the pleadings of the Bank Customer Action Collective, just the same as he had stonewalled the Cork Business man's pleadings in 1997.

Obviously this was the Don's modus operandi.

Just say nothing and deny everything seems to be a common strategy of the big boys, or as we are finding out at the UK inquiry memory loss also seems to be quite prevalent in the executive handbook when direct questions are asked.

Individuals appointed to high positions of power who believe they are entitled to make such unscrupulous decisions to deliberately destroy people's lives, simply to shut them up, the way the head of the UK Post Office and the CEO of Nab have done; surely has got no part in our free world.

Any fair thinking individual would have to agree that the action Don Argus chose to follow was a totally inhuman act that proved he and the corporate he was the head of had no intension to uphold the obligations that all corporate citizens in a free world must abide by.

This Mr Big was obviously above the rule of law.

The bank had actually set about deliberately engineering the legal system in order to undermine the sanctity of the High

Court process. An action that was a serious breach of the Bank of New Zealand's conditions of its registration that is held by the Reserve Bank of New Zealand, but this serious breach was not reprimanded under prudential conditions of the Reserve Bank Act as it would have been in a fair and just society.

An official complaint was laid under the prudential and registration conditions of the Reserve Bank Act by the BCAC with the Reserve Bank and the Minister of Finance, but sadly no mandated action was taken by them.

Apparently a New Zealand Registered Bank has immunity from prosecution for breaking the laws that the common people are thrown in jail for.

The Sub Postmasters in the UK were prosecuted for false accounting and theft, so why not a Bank?

Prima facie' evidence identifies the fact that the BNZ had systematically stolen money from their customers account in such a way the loaded interest charges would be very hard to detect.

Isn't that false accounting to effect a theft/fraud?

It is known that the lawyer who was working for the BNZ in the Eatwell case (including the failed strike out action heard by Master Thomas) had at a later time written a paper (and ran seminars) to a nation-wide lawyers publication and web page, detailing how to employ insolvency actions against property owners to intercept the justice process that may be accessed via legal aid.

Furthermore, even though in NZ they were unaware of the situation at the time, it is indisputable that Don Argus had full knowledge that his two banks had been stealing off their customers, and these customers had long running disputes with the bank based on it. However even with this knowledge he allowed the Bank and its lawyers to continue with its threatening tactics to the customers who had dared to complain, and going to the extent of failing to cooperate with the Banking Ombudsman, probably with the intention of avoiding being exposed to public scrutiny the way the Irish bank had been.

It is also quite chilling to realize that Don Argus was a member of the board of directors on both of the Nab owned Bank of New Zealand and the National Irish Bank at the time these events were taking place and yet he allowed people's lives to keep being destroyed by his bank, furthermore, it is particularly vile to learn from the Irish High Court report that the illegal practices uncovered had been Nab policies that were introduced in the 1980's in the drive to increase their new off -shore banks market share to boost the profit line.

The same practice has been heard at the UK Post Office inquiry where Paula Vennels ex CEO of the Post Office has been exposed as wittingly allowing sub Post Masters to be wrongly charged and imprisoned for theft (or giving in to suicide) rather than admitting errors in the very costly Horizon Computer system that had been installed in the Post Office system in 1999.

Accordingly the most likely chain of events following Don Argus receiving the Bank Customer Action Collective's (BCAC) letter was that he instructed Mike Pratt CEO of BNZ to shut these people down quickly.

While it is also important to note that the Irish High Court report stated that NIB was still being very aggressive and obstructive to the Irish High Court inspectors at the time and they only came into line when the Irish High Court directed them to cooperate in January 1999.

It is internationally known that the Nab is very aggressive in the way it conducts its business, so it would be typical to expect that when the BCAC wrote to the Don he was still arrogant enough to be thinking he was going to squash the Irish High Court investigation.

Wrong Don; the Irish High Court had a different plan.

The Irish High Court changed that, but the New Zealand High Court and the Government did nothing and were soundly defeated by the Australian aggression.

Under this mind-set it would be logical that they would think shutting down the possibility of the problem spilling over into their New Zealand bank could be achieved by sending in the receivers to the Eatwell farms. It would be fair to make this assumption with what we know now, because this type of reaction was consistent with the bank's other bully boy actions being felt by complaining bank customers in general throughout New Zealand, Ireland and Australia at the time.

There have been numerous reports/films and protests aired that have exposed the same human carnage directly caused by the same draconian tactics being imposed on Australian Customers of Nab that would substantiate the conclusions made about the uncouth game the Don was playing.

There was a Royal Commission of Inquiry undertaken in Australia that substantiates the claims made by Australian bank customers who were crushed by the all powerful bankers.

Obviously the Australian public would have been up in arms if they knew that Nab was being just as brutal to their off shore banks customers, therefore as Nab is a major player in the Australian four pillar banking structure, the hard ball tactics to shut the BCAC and the Eatwells down would have been a typical strategy followed by Don Argus at the time.

Throughout the prolonged battle that followed all the directors of the BNZ have been written to personally and informed of their banks overcharging and other illegal practices, and after 2004 when the Paul Appleby report was finally published further pleadings were made to the BNZ directors simply asking that the travesty of their banks behaviour should be properly heard.

Amazingly the BNZ board of directors included Pamela Jefferies who had been the Chief Human Rights Commissioner when she was recruited to the banks board of Directors and even she ignored the principle that customers had the common law right to a just hearing.

Subsequently the Chief Human Rights Commissioner Rosslyn Noonan and other commissioners at the Human Rights Commission did try to help the Eatwell's with their petitions to Parliament and with other advice only to be totally ignored by the whole Select Committee process including Parliamentary staff and the elected members of Parliament.

It adds insult to injury to realize that Pamela Jefferies would have been head hunted for the Banks Board of directors to give a false public impression of the bank's societal integrity.

By the official snubbing of the Human Rights Commission's advice in the way Parliament has done, the commission has been exposed as being unable to be effective in its mandate and in so doing has seriously magnified the Governments failings to honour its Human Rights obligations of State as per the United Nations Human Rights committee's directive.

The Nab bank had bought the Irish bank off the Midland bank in 1986 and changed its name from the Northern Bank to the National Irish Bank. It was well known in Ireland that Nab had set about shaking up the Irish Banking Industry. Commonly it was said in Ireland that the bank from down under expected a profitable return on its new investment and so NIB became the most outwardly aggressive bank in pursuit of market share in Ireland.

The BNZ went through the same phase in the early 90's and it was from the aggressive marketing and promises made by the bank during that drive for new business that the Eatwell companies banking business accounts were moved to the BNZ's Nelson branch in 1993. In the book "You can Bank on it" this "partnership" is framed as a marriage to be consistent with the banks sales pitch.

Bankers employed by NIB told the Irish High Court's investigating officers that they had taken instruction in interest-loading by their superiors in the bank and it was made clear to the inspectors that the practice was simply an exercise to increase the profitability of the branch and that result could ultimately generate personal bonuses when good returns were achieved from the aggressive practices they were applying.

National Australia Bank took ownership of the Bank of New Zealand and incorporated the Bank of New Zealand Limited on the New Zealand Companies register on 14th March 1989.

Ross Pinney has been a director of the BNZ during three different periods, which appear to coincide with situations when pressure was being applied about the banks antics and when you note the role he played in the NIB exposure we can assume he has been a trouble shooter or a moderator on the BNZ board during those times. Surely Director Jefferies would have taken some convincing at times.

The banks lawyers did write and growl about the directors being contacted directly, but that bluff and bluster was made in total disregard of the purpose of Company Directors being available, as laid down by the Companies office.

Yet another lawyer breaking the law.

For a director to have their contact details excluded from a company's registration details there has to be a legitimate reason given to the Companies Office to allow this to happen.

Don Argus had been a director of the BNZ from November 1992 until 22nd January 1999 about when the Irish High Court got on top of their nonsense in Ireland. He obviously knew too much and the Irish High Court investigators were going after the Directors of NIB and Don Argus was one of them.

It is well known that following the take-over of the BNZ the Nab sent its own team of officers to the branches around New Zealand with rousing presentations to motivate the staff to think the Nab way, just the same as they had done in Ireland in the 1980's. Therefore there is little doubt that the process that the Irish investigation identified would have been pretty much the same process that was applied to convert the Bank of New Zealand employees to the Nab way. The pitch that followed was very similar to the Cork Business man's description of the sales presentation style he encountered in Ireland.

As a point of interest, in 1998/99 the CEO of BNZ was Mike Pratt who was an Australian.

Excerpt from the Irish High Court report.

January 1999: The Supreme Court orders NIB employees to co-operate with the investigation of High Court inspectors because of the seriousness of allegations.

Culture and Operational Environment

We consider it important to set the conclusions of our report in relation to tax evasion in the context of the culture of the period the subject of our investigation. This was highlighted in the report of the Committee of Public Accounts following their enquiry into DIRT, published in December 1999. The problem of DIRT evasion was an industry-wide phenomenon.

The operational environment in the Bank at the time has also to be taken into account and the behavior of individual branch managers and staff must be viewed in this context. The branch network was target driven - there were, amongst others, targets for fee income and deposits, but limited support by way of systems or training to enable the achievement of these targets. Managers felt under pressure to meet these targets, in the setting of which they had negligible participation and which many considered unreasonable; they feared criticism and possible humiliation before their fellow managers if they did not meet the targets set.

While many branch managers operated, or played a part in, the improper practices, we have concluded that it would be inappropriate to find individual managers responsible, as we believe that responsibility for the practices lay at a higher level in the Bank. We must add also that we received no evidence that branch managers personally derived any direct financial benefit from the operation of any of the practices.

Summary Conclusions - Responsibility

We have concluded that responsibility for the improper practices which existed rests with senior management of the Bank during the period covered by the investigations.

It was their duty to ensure that the business of the Bank was so conducted that such practices did not occur and, if they did, that they were stopped immediately.

We have also concluded that the Head of the Bank's Financial Advice and Services Division, and a number of the financial services managers in that Division, were responsible for the promotion of the CMI policies as a secure investment for funds undisclosed to the Revenue.
We have also considered the discharge of their functions by the following:

- the Bank's internal audit;
- the external auditors to the Bank;
- the Audit Committee of the Board, and
- the Board of Directors.

The Irish High Court Director of Corporate Enforcement Paul Appleby warned of social disruption and economic damage if high profile white collar crimes are not punished and he went on to prosecute 9 of the NIB directors and officials achieving some very long winded prosecutions. It is amazing that the 9 directors and/or officials did not include Don Argus as he was obviously a key director and clearly a highly influential member of the board, so it is an interesting dilemma particularly when the consideration of the fact that the Irish High Court investigation had exposed that the illegal practices of NIB was a culture that bank employees had claimed to have been introduced by the parent bank Nab, soon after it had taken over the bank and renamed it, thus becoming their new employer. The reported training given to the employees of NIB by Nab to increase the profit line had necessitated the illegal practices that were under investigation. Maybe the "social disruption and economic damage" warnings only applied to the Irish white collar criminals involved in Paul Appleby's thinking at the time. Australians didn't count even though the report had concluded that the illegal practices were encouraged by the Australian owners.

Given the dishonesty of the most senior executives involved it is unthinkable that both Don Argus and Ross Pinney went on to be very influential in Australian business circles where

Don Argus was honoured as a senior fellow of Financial Services institute of Australia and Ross Pinney was President of Red Cross of Australia and was awarded a distinguished service medal from Red Cross in 2015. Ross Pinney was also on 5 different Charitable Organisations and the chairman of the Rural Bank Limited.

From all that has subsequently been revealed it is obvious that the hierarchy of the BNZ (including their lawyers) had to be aware of the Irish High Court action being taken against the sibling bank NIB for interest overcharging that had been adjudged to be theft and they knew that Eatwell Livestock Limited and Eatwell Hospitality Limited had filed a claim against the bank in the NZ High Court that included the damage caused by the banks overcharging practice.

In defiance of the Court the Bank set about undermining it, by continuing with the destructive actions they were taking on the Eatwell business, while they kept on pulling the wool over the eyes of the Banking Ombudsman, the High Court, Government Officials and any other prying eyes they encountered.

It worked- the Eatwell family lost everything.

NIB Timeline: The High Court Inspectors' report was six years in the making. Here are the main events that led to the uncovering of the extent of corruption at the bank.

- **June 1998:** Former NIB employee Ms Beverly Flynn, a Fianna Fáil TD at the time, is named as one of the people who sold financial products that facilitated tax evasion. She announces she will sue RTÉ for libel. The High Court extends investigation to cover National Irish Bank Financial Services.
- Settle its liability for failing to collect DIRT tax from customers, after a damning report from the Dáil Public Accounts Committee.
- **January 2001:**NIB offers settlements to the 470 customers who bought offshore investment bonds in the Clerical Medical International policies in the Isle of Man. The customers were encouraged to buy the bonds, which were then put on deposit with NIB in Ireland. No capital gains tax was paid because the money was in the name of the offshore company.
- **April 2001:**Fianna Fail TD Beverly-Cooper Flynn loses her libel case against RTÉ but appeals to the Supreme Court.
- **May 2001:**NIB admits the scandal has cost it €22 million and 27 years' worth of work hours to date.
- **July 2002:** Interim report compiled by the inspectors is presented to the High Court.
- **August 2003:**A draft copy of the final High Court inspectors' report is provided to the NIB, which is invited to respond.
- **March 2004:** The bank furnishes its response.
- **April 2004:** Beverly Cooper-Flynn loses her Supreme Court appeal against RTÉ and is expelled from the Fianna Fáil party.
- **July 2004:** The final inspectors' report into the NIB affair is presented to the High Court and the Director

of Corporate Enforcement, Paul Appleby. The report is not made available to any other parties.

- **Last Friday:** After objections in the High Court from several parties, Mr Justice Peter Kelly directs that the 400-page NIB report be published in full. More than €50 million has already been paid over to the Revenue Commissioners by individuals settling tax liabilities arising from the NIB CMI scheme.

Chapter 5

Contempt of Court perverts justice.

Bankers use Insolvency laws as a weapon.

The case Eatwell Livestock Limited and Eatwell Hospitality Limited Vs Bank of New Zealand claim was filed in the High Court Greymouth (shifted to Wellington later) in 1998 as a desperate measure when the BNZ continued with its abusive culture, irrespective of a long campaign of letter writing, some kangaroo court style meetings, and pleadings for fairness and justice from the Prime Minister, Members of Parliament, Banking Ombudsman and many others.

The claim sited illegal charges that had been made against the company's bank accounts amounting to many thousands of dollars over several years and the costly dispute that followed. The bank had ridiculed the Eatwell's complaints about the effects of the overcharging practice that culminated in the quantified claim exceeding $900,000 being lodged with the High Court.

However, the reaction of the bank was to apply to the High Court to have the claim struck out. Unfortunately for the bank when this action was heard in the High Court at

Wellington by Master Thomas the judgment went against the banks action to strike the claim out, sighting that to strike the claim out would not serve justice.

In a letter to the Eatwells instructing lawyer the Auckland Barrister Iain Hutcheson who acted in the High Court case said *"I do believe that Counsel for the BNZ misunderstood the legal position, and the extensive research from overseas authority, which I provided to Master Thomas, which led him to comment that he felt that he had decided some of the prior similar applications incorrectly. I am therefore confident of success."*

Mr Hutcheson's summation was correct, Master Thomas ruled that the evidence just had to be heard giving the opportunity for witnesses to be cross examined for justice to be served.

It would have been very interesting to see the bankers on the stand to be cross examined because they relied heavily on the bluff and bluster tactics keeping them out of the Court and struggled to understand the complexities of their own malpractices.

The bullish tactics worked and Master Thomas's judgment was overridden.

Subsequently the judgement came before another Court action in defence of a case where another claim was being challenged to be struck out, where the Master Thomas High Court Judgment was applied sighting Master Thomas's judgment as being that to be the rule as set down by Sian Elias Chief Justice to be the principle to be applied, as per Court records, as follows:

The rule was amended in 1998 by adding (b) to allow a defendant to apply for summary judgement. In Eatwell Livestock Ltd v BNZ 13 PRNZ 671 the master said that in the summary judgment jurisdiction the interests of justice required that there be caution when considering a defendant's application. That is because, if for no other reason, a successful summary judgment by a defendant will result in issue estoppel. The Court of Appeal has recently delivered its first judgment in respect of the amended rule. It endorses the Master's approach in Eatwell. See Westpac Banking Corporation and ANZ Banking Group v N.M.Kembla NZ Limited CA 50/00 & CA51/00 judgment 9/11/2000.

The principles to be applied are set out in judgment of the Court delivered by Elias CJ (p21 et seq):

However the BNZ proceeded to take action under insolvency laws to put the Eatwell Companies into receivership based on a falsely calculated default, in direct defiance of the judgment of Master Thomas who made it clear that his judgment was made in "the interests of justice" to prevent the case resulting "in issue estoppel".

By giving no regard to the High Court a perversion of the due course of justice was committed by the BNZ's lawyer when an application to have the Eatwell Companies assets sold up was made with full knowledge of the claim that had been filed in the High Court against the BNZ, and would be fully aware that if the claim was successful it would prove that the Eatwells were not in breach of the contracts held with the BNZ in any case.

Given the scenario whereby if the Eatwells High Court claim was heard the BNZ would have no legal right to sell the Eatwells property in any case, but the banks illegal practices would have been exposed.

In other words regardless of the outcome of the case the bank would still lose because the evidence would expose the crimes the bank had committed.

The application to appoint a receiver was also taken in direct defiance of the principle of Justice as adjudged by the Chief

Justice Sian Elias stating the principle to be applied was to "endorse the Masters approach in *Eatwell*".

In defiance of the Chief Justice the BNZ took pre-emptive actions that were deliberately implemented to intercept the High Court process. Clearly the only possible need to rush the process through was to hide the illegality that would be exposed to the Court when the complexities of the overcharging practices were cross examined.

Following the receivership the property was sold by the receiver and the Eatwell family were evicted under direct threat of arrest imposed by a large contingent of armed police on 30th May 1999, following which the Eatwell's made it publically known they intended to continue with the High Court claim.

Following the High Court strike out action failure the Bank conspired with one of the company's creditors, Pyne Gould Guinness who held personal guarantees over Gray and Vickie Eatwell and convinced them to take action to bankrupt them.

Consequently, on 16th October 2000 Gray and Vickie Eatwell were adjudged bankrupt by the High Court Master Venning in the Christchurch Court.

Following the bankruptcy hearing on 18th October 2000 a
letter from Deloitte Touche Tohmatsu was sent to Gerald
Sare, Bank of New Zealand Wellington, enclosing a notice
which was to be published in the Christchurch Press on the
19th October 2000.

The receivers letter went on to say *"We understand from
people present in the Court at the time that Mr & Mrs
Eatwell endeavoured to debate the issue with Master
Venning and were removed from the court."* This statement
was totally untrue and obviously intended to discredit the
Eatwells. In fact during the hearing Master Venning spoke
directly to Mr Eatwell who stood up and informed the
Master about the High Court Claim in the Wellington High
Court that was awaiting a hearing date to be set. The Master
looked down at his notes, but the lawyer acting for Pyne
Gould Guinness bounced up and told the Master that one of
the Eatwell Company claims had been struck out by Master
Thomas in the High Court and that the other company claim
would not be likely to succeed.

The question that should be asked would be, as it was nearly
two years after the Receivers had been appointed why the
Receiver would think that the BNZ would be interested in the
Bankruptcy of the Eatwells, specifically as the BNZ had no
personal claim against Gray and Vickie Eatwell and stood to
gain nothing.

Oh yes, the claim that the bank had just overridden in contempt of the High Court to hide their crimes.

The truth actually proves that the lawyers misleading statement was in contempt of Court and would constitute perjury at the best, because at the end of the strike out hearing in Wellington an arrangement was made with Master Thomas, Iain Hutcheson (Eatwell's Barrister) and Gray and Vickie Eatwell that one company name would be removed from the claim to assist the Court by avoiding the need to double up in every Court document and just waste time.

This agreement is evidenced in the Court notices printed above naming Eatwell Livestock Limited Vs BNZ when the claim had originally been filed and heard by Master Thomas in both company names.

It is most likely that the Pynes lawyer had made a false statement to Master Venning because he had not actually studied the facts of the case, if indeed he had done his preparation that he should have done before addressing the Court, because if he had he would have been conscious he was breaking the law. However in this case the crime the lawyer committed was a reckless omission of the truth.

The ramifications of the negligence directly caused to the Eatwells were horrendous.

Furthermore, the hurried processes that were applied by the Master that day resulted in an indictment on the Courts mandate to deliver natural justice to all citizens that are being charged before them. Simply put, the Law Courts doctrine is to ensure that a defendant's common law rights are observed at all times, however in this case the Courts procedures failed to deliver the citizens fundamental right to be heard.

Based on a lawyer giving the Master incorrect information there was a serious miscarriage of justice committed by the Court and surely the lawyer should have been sanctioned and/or struck off.

During the hearing before Master Thomas in Wellington the Eatwell's Barrister had explained to the Master that the case put by the banks lawyer that set out to belittle the integrity of the Eatwell business by shrugging them off as being in a hopeless position. However in order to disprove this charade Mr Hutcheson presented some basic facts that had previously not been seen by the Court. It only took the Master being shown the statement that demonstrated that the Eatwells had bought equity of $2.1m to the table when taking up finance contracts with the BNZ in 1993, which demonstrated to him that the degrading tactic of the banks lawyer, was just that; a derogatory tactic intended to mislead the Court.

The agreed strategy to defend the strike out action was to keep our cards close to the chest so as not to lose the advantage we held over the banks defence of the claim.

We had all the facts and figures, but the bankers were in a muddle.

Iain Hutcheson's case to defend the strike out action was to focus on the need for justice to be the priority, rather than show the intricate details of the claim against the bank.

Subsequent to these events Members of Parliament and other authorities to whom the Eatwells continued calling on to deliver them the fundamental right to be heard, were being told by the BNZ and their henchmen (lobbyists) that the High Court claim would not have succeeded anyway and were suggesting that the judgment of Master Thomas was wrong. This dishonest approach was in contempt of Parliament, particularly with the fact that during the High Court hearing Master Thomas had been shown enough information for him to comment to Mr Hutcheson that he felt that he had decided some of the prior similar applications incorrectly.

 A judge would not make such a confession to a barrister in Court if there was any indication that the case before him was groundless and a waste of the High Court's time.

The proof of the true position is found in the Court records.

Jason Beer KC the Counsel to the inquiry into the UK Post Office scandal currently running (April/May 2024) told Lawyer Jamail Singh that the beguile of his answers to the questions put to him were a "Big Fat Lie" and Rodrick Williams who was under oath was told "I suggest you are lying". Therefore we can only wonder what Jason Beer KC would have to say to the Pyne Gould Guinness lawyer.

Isn't a lawyer deliberately misleading the Judge in Court a crime?

In defence of Master Venning he had adjudged the Eatwells bankrupt in the absence of the truth about the status of the Eatwell High Court claim before him; however he could not have adjudged the Eatwells as bankrupts, if he was in possession of the full facts about the Eatwells High Court claim. In the absence of the truth the Master had perverted the high standard of justice principles required of the High Court process.

It is nearly impossible to get a lawyer to defend a bankruptcy case because at such a time when you've been cleaned out for a year you have no money to pay a lawyer.

That's what happened to Gray and Vickie Eatwell - No money - No lawyer- No justice.

No freedom of speech either.

Following the untrue statement of the lawyer Mr Eatwell did try to explain the facts to Master Venning, but the Master ignored him. According to the receiver Bruce McAlister's letter to the banker, *"Mr & Mrs Eatwell endeavoured to debate the issue with Master Venning and were removed from the court."*

When did a person facing a charge in Court have their right to free speech removed?

How the Court can justify treating any person before them who is facing total ruin without allowing them their right to be heard is a serious indictment on the principles of Justice that lay at the foundation of the whole legal system.

The Court was full of people with a long bench of mostly young lawyers because a lot of cases were to be heard in that session, so it would be reasonable to conclude that Master Venning was more focussed on getting through them all rather than maintaining the high moral standard of justice expected of the judiciary in New Zealand.

The Courts attitudes towards people facing insolvency are disgusting and support the shocking behaviour that the banks use as their weapon.

Freedom of speech – Yeah Right!

Mr McAlister (receiver) of Deloitte Touche Tohmatsu also lied (and or maliciously misled) Gerald Sare at the BNZ in his letter to the BNZ by saying Mr and Mrs Eatwell were removed from the court, because even though Mr and Mrs Eatwell were highly stressed and in a state of total disbelief that this injustice could be happening to them, other than the endeavour to inform Master Venning of the truth and the travesty to justice being imposed on them; they acted with professionalism and left the Court quietly.

Some of their friends present were quite distraught at the result and did protest.

The perversion that followed was that at the first opportunity Stephen Tubbs of BDO the Court appointed Official Assignee orchestrated the filing of a notice of discontinuance of the Eatwell Livestock v BNZ claim in the High Court, without the legal authority to do so.

"Issue estoppel" was achieved! Rich law had defeated common law and natural justice.

As bankrupts and totally broken the Eatwell's had no means to fight the injustice that had been dumped on them and went on to try and find justice from the highest Court in the land, the Government.

Something must be drastically wrong with the justice system when the Prime Minister couldn't do anything about the

Eatwell's case with the BNZ because it was "before the Court", but the BNZ was able to use insolvency laws to override the High Court process that was awaiting a trial date.

Obviously In New Zealand - Rich law defeats common law, specifically where a principle of justice as stated by the Chief Justice can be ignored by Lawyers and the Courts when big money people are involved, and worst of all is that there is no affordable course of redress to those that become the victims of evil intent when justice is so easily defeated by the power of money.

They take your money and then you can't afford justice.

The Government was prepared to allow a registered bank to negate a citizen's rights to a just hearing, while the Courts and the Government wittingly stood by and allowed this to happen. They had been coerced into standing by and making a complete mockery of the principles identified by the Chief Justice's judgment that was made with Justice as the highest principle.

New Zealand's Government has failed to uphold the Universal Declaration of Human Rights by the deliberate betrayal of a citizen's access to the statutory right to the protection from oppression by the rule of law.

This example of injustice must in some way highlight a major threat to New Zealand's justice system.

Gray Eatwell has said in many media statements that he would continue to fight for the right to justice at every level he could find in New Zealand. For many years he has done so, but no justice has been delivered.

West Coast Times

Phone 755 8422, Fax 755 8204, PO Box 122 Hokitika
135th year of publication

MONDAY MAY 31, 1999
Price 45c

Evicted farmer vows fight

Embattled Franz Josef farmer Gray Eatwell and wife Vickie, were evicted from their farm yesterday and are now homeless.

Mr Eatwell was issued with a trespass order on Saturday by the police who threatened arrest if he did not leave the $2 million property before their midday yesterday departure deadline.

The Franz Josf property has been sold by receivers working on behalf of the Bank of New Zealand but Mr Eatwell claims to have documented evidence which he said suggests the bank acted improperly while selling his farm.

Mr Eatwell's son-in-law, who is currently managing the farm, will also be forced to leave the land no later than Tuesday as part of a negotiated deal with a receivership representative.

Large police numbers gathered in Franz Josef for the eviction. Mr Eatwell said rather than resorting to violence he chose to leave his farm peacefully and vowed to fight on in the courts.

"Our position was we would not get violent. They made it clear to us we would be arrested if we did not leave and we were booted out," he said.

Mr Eatwell said the saga has been at huge personal cost to him and his family and he said he now had "no place to go".

"We had no other option, we have done everything possible within the law but we have been dealt a mean blow. We are shattered."

Mr Eatwell said he would stay with family until future arrangements were made and he said he now has nothing to lose and remained steadfast to his belief he has been wronged.

"We will fight on but we have not got a lot of money like the banks to fight in court. That is what's frightening us."

The legal battle was still before the High Court, with no hearing date set, Mr Eatwell told NZPA yesterday.

Despite that, the bank brought in the receivers, and sold the farm by tender. The new owners took possession on Friday.

The family had intended to stay for as long as it could, knowing that once they left, and new owners moved in, there was little chance of returning.

When police told them that they could leave peacefully, or be arrested, they chose the former.

"We're desperate people, but we're not law-breakers," Mr Eatwell said.

Though the farm had been lost, that would not end the matter.

"We're not going to give up, I can tell you that quite categorically. We never ever wanted to be fighting for money but it looks like we are," he said.

Homeless. Vickie and Gray Eatwell with one of the signs they used to protest against their eviction.

Timberlands prai

Timberlands West Coast manager
techniques have won furth

British Colum
Schrol
vi

"My wife and I . . . my family, we've lost everything, so we're pretty p.... off. We've been over a pretty hard road, we've just got to swallow it."

Arguments that the farm should not be sold until the court action was resolved had been ignored, and Mr Eatwell felt the system had failed his family.

"We feel we've been run over by a bulldozer, to be quite honest. We've fought as hard as we can, we've been as high as the Prime Minister."

Prime Minister Jenny Shipley had said she could not get involved while it was before the courts, Mr Eatwell said.

The Eatwells alleged that the BNZ had crippled them through inaccurate financial calculations. They were customers of the bank's Nelson branch.

Mr Eatwell has a claim in the High Court in Greymouth against the BNZ, seeking more than $900,000 in overcharged interest, subsequent loss of income, and costs in recovering money owed.

Chapter 6

Meeting ex PM Jenny Shipley:

Gray and Vickie Eatwell had made many trips to Parliament and on this occasion they parked their car in the visitor's car parks that used to be in front of the beehive. They had made so many trips to Parliament over the years that on one occasion there were no visitor parks available where they normally parked, but as they were about to drive back out of the grounds a security guard came quickly over to them and said no worries, you can use the VIP car park, you are VIP's. The security guard said you guys do come here a lot don't you. Gray and Vickie thanked him for his help and locked the car.

They actually had quite a few interesting times driving into the grand entrance of Parliament; one real interesting occasion was soon after 9/11 when the security people ran bomb detectors under the car before they were allowed to go over to where they normally parked in front of the Beehive.

On this day in March 2002 they made their way to the main doors of the old Parliament building. Vickie was wearing a new outfit their daughter had made for her and looked pretty smart, so they went into the building and were directed to the Office of the Member of Parliament they were meeting that day.

They were met by a nice PA lady at reception who led them along one of the corridors in the grand old building to where they were ushered into a small meeting room with the offer of a cup of tea. Then in a short time the lady they were meeting breezed in. She too wore a smart dress suit, but hers was blue. As they sat down Gray quipped "it is always nice when pen pals meet isn't it", as the Ex- Prime Minister Jenny Shipley sat down in front of them with a smile of agreement.

It was March 2002 and at the last general election there had been a change of Government and Mrs Shipley was no longer the Prime Minister, but had agreed to meet with the Eatwell's following a discussion on talk back radio where Mrs Shipley had told the nation she had got it wrong when the Eatwells had asked for help with their situation with the BNZ. On talk back radio she had explained to the listeners that she did nothing at the time because she thought it was a "witch hunt".

That isn't what the letters had said during the period when she was still the Prime Minister though.

The meeting was frank but friendly and Mrs Shipley made a solemn apology to them both saying she would try to help them if she could while she was still an MP in Parliament, because as she said "it happened on my watch and I'm very sorry".

The apology was accepted with grace, but sadly left a very empty feeling in Gray and Vickie's hearts. If only she had done something way back when she could have, like on 12th

April 1999 when they had written to her as the Prime Minister as they had many times. In her reply to that letter on 21st May 1999 the PM wrote that she considered the approach to the Banking Ombudsman was the appropriate course of action, but went on to say *"I understand that you are also pursuing legal action in relation to your concerns over your dealings with the Bank of New Zealand. If this is the case, it would not be appropriate for me to comment on the details of your case."*

The police arrived 10 days later on 31st May 1999 with a 15 officer strong force with armed offender's squad, paddy wagons, with officers armed with pepper spray, batons, (not drawn) with fire arms available (as per police report) and threw the Eatwells out of their homes and off their land.

In total disrespect of the Banking Ombudsman and the legal action filed in the High Court.

If this is the result of taking an *"appropriate course of action"* then the Prime Minister must have been presiding over in a foreign land when she said that.

It is very confusing that the Prime Minister was not able to act due to the claim lodged in the High Court and bowed out, (or was it a cop out?) but the BNZ was able to ignore the "legal action" in the High Court and proceeded to take the Eatwells out, with the backing of the New Zealand police force to over-ride the High Court and the common laws of the land that they had solemnly sworn to enforce.

Even though the police officers were sympathetic to the Eatwells in person they had acted with full knowledge of the legal status of the ownership of the property, if not before they arrived at the property, they had to go past the signs that were erected stating that *"The ownership of this property is subject to High Court Action".*

Rich law had defeated common law again.

After the Eatwells had been evicted from their property there was an internal email sent by Gerald Sare (a senior executive from the Asset Recovery branch of the bank), to Mike Pratt the CEO of BNZ, thanking him for his "support" on the day of the police action.

Was that support to instruct the police or maybe to pay someone?

We are not sure what "support" the CEO of a large Australia owned bank could have applied that resulted in the High Court being overridden, but the status of the High Court had no jurisdiction that day.

While still the Prime Minister Mrs Shipley had written to the Eatwells quite often, but following her receiving a copy of his book that was published the year before, she had said *"You can Bank on it" – is very well written – a hard story to write -* included within her letter of thanks for the copy of the book given as a gift/koha.

At the photo shoot with Bill Deed, old Pine Tree couldn't stop muttering "I'm not a hooker, I'm a lock". Even though Colin was in his 60's then he was still a big man and he felt like an ox under my arm when we went into the front row scrum pose.

Having read the book the Ex-Prime Minister had a pretty good knowledge of the battle that burdened them, while the Eatwells and other customers of the BNZ, some featuring in the book have fought on seeking justice.

The Bank Customer Action Collective was contacted by many disenfranchised BNZ customers following media coverage, however in the absence of an investigation commensurate with the Irish High Court there is no way of knowing how many customers of the BNZ had been ripped off and the money has wandered off to some shareholders pocket in Australia or maybe further abroad.

With the impressions and the knowledge gained from frequent communications with Mrs Shipley as Prime Minister over the years and having personally discussed the deep feeling of betrayal that was burdening them, it is hard not to wonder what she might be thinking now that she has been charged for her own breaches to the conditions of the Companies Act as a Director of Mainzeal.

Unfortunately Mrs Shipley has been prosecuted for failing to uphold her obligations to the statutory conditions of the Companies Act that a company director must comply with and has subsequently been directed by the Court to pay millions of dollars in restitution.

The Supreme Court judgment of the Mainzeal case declared the finding as being *"of fundamental importance to the business community"* which was clearly intended to send a signal to company directors at large to be fully aware of their legal responsibilities and liabilities when they take up the cushy sounding company directorships on offer.

The New Zealand Supreme Court finding is not unlike Irish Director of Corporate Enforcement Paul Appleby who stated that if white collar crime is not arrested there would be "social disruption and economic damage as a result".

There is a broadly held belief that Mrs Shipley was sucked into a false sense of security while she was an MP and Prime Minister, particularly watching how the old Boys and Girls club (Ex PM's and ex MP's etc) swanned around raking in very handsome sums in director's fees from their books of directorships and this must have had a rosy appeal as being a good opportunity to pursue after her retirement from Parliament.

As New Zealand's Prime Minister Mrs Shipley had rubbed shoulders with many so called top business people, like Kerry McDonald (Ex-Chairman of the Board of BNZ) who was directly involved in batting off the Eatwells and any official investigation into the overcharging and other practices of the BNZ.

On one occasion Mr McDonald was directly involved with John Wright MP of the Alliance Party, when Mr Wright had tried very hard to arrange a meeting for the Eatwells with him as the chairman of the bank's board of directors, specifically to give them an opportunity to present their concerns to him. Unfortunately in one such episode when Mr McDonald dismissed the pleadings being made to him quite aggressively had transpired during a phone conversation, while the Eatwells were in Mr Wrights Parliamentary office. (Listening on a speaker phone)

What was said and the tone of its delivery was quite upsetting for the Eatwells, so Mr Wright quickly turned the speaker off. They had heard enough to give them a very hollow feeling of disappointment which Mr Wright had seen on their faces.

The hidden overcharging practice and the effect it was having on the severe actions being imposed by his bank were reported to him by the Eatwells and other customers of his bank. But contrary to the man's very high image in the corporate world Mr McDonald used his influence to oppose external investigations into the illicit practices being reported to him. Submissions were made at many levels of authority including the Government; but his reactions were reminiscent to those of Paula Vennells (ex CEO of the UK Post Office) who has been exposed obfuscating the facts to forensic investigators, Select Committees etc, as it has now been exposed in the official inquiry currently running in Westminster.

Mr McDonald mimicked the corporate culture of arrogance adopted by Paula Vennells.

The more that the attitude of top management is being publically exposed in the UK and elsewhere around the globe it very much points to a corporate culture that the company image and shareholders dividends are more important than the law of the land. Anything goes, while no qualms are given to the callous actions taken to tear people's lives apart, are being justified in the executive mind with an air of superiority that the Company (money) comes first at all cost, as it has been done by the UK Post Office; it has been mirrored in New Zealand corporates.

Unfortunately the same corporate mind-set is the modus operandi of many of the executives of the New Zealand Government and Official offices of compliance.

All the Eatwells wanted was to discuss how they had discovered the overcharging practices and how the practice has now been identified as being identical to bank practices that the Irish High Court has found to be theft/fraud in the case of the NIB. Unfortunately the Eatwells were still naive enough to believe that any right thinking person would realize they were right to complain and "put it right". Therefore it is quite astounding and somewhat disgusting to realise that Mr McDonald would have been fully aware of the Irish High Court investigation into those same practices at the time, but of course he knew, but the Eatwells didn't.

Obviously the Board's chairman would have to know because of nothing else but the fact that Don Argus and Ross Pinney were personally involved in the NIB case in Ireland and they were directors on the Board of BNZ at the same time.

All of the directors knew about the BNZ's overcharging practice because the Eatwells had written to every one of them at their home address as recorded on the Companies Office official register.

It is of some significance that the Irish High Court officially advised the Reserve Bank of New Zealand of the findings in the investigation into NIB, but of course the Reserve Bank doesn't do prudential supervision of the Banks they register under conditions of the Reserve Bank Act like they are mandated to.

Abdication of statutory duty.

Kerry McDonald is one of those with the high profile individuals having been awarded the title of New Zealand Executive of the year in 1996; hence he quickly climbed up the ladder of top business people moving and shaking all and sundry. He even got the nod from the National Australia Bank for a cushy directorship over there at one time.

In 2019 having been hailed as one of New Zealand's most experienced Directors Kerry McDonald was reported as having expressed concerns about issues with governance standards within the Banking Industry, when he called for an official commission of inquiry into banking management standards following the sudden resignation of the Australia New Zealand Bank (ANZ) chief executive.

Given he had such a high status, it is sickening to recall that 20 years earlier Kerry McDonald, as the head of the governance of the BNZ went to great lengths to block the call for an official investigation into the BNZ's shocking actions, so what's changed?

Hypocrisy to the max.

Chapter 7

Farm Debt Mediation Bill

In the Mr Bates Vs the Post Office scandal there was a time in 2013-2015 that a mediation process had been operating, but unfortunately the system was a total failure that simply became a smoke screen that gave victims of the Post Office some false hope, but in reality the UK Post Office just carried on and gave the mediators and the sub Post Masters the single finger salute.

In New Zealand Members of Parliament assisting the Eatwells efforts to find an effective remedy for their claims of the BNZ's malpractice had also tried to introduce a Farm Debt Mediation Bill to Parliament.

Initially John Wright MP discussed the idea with the Eatwells explaining that such systems exist in other countries and it was thought this process would at least expose some of the unfair practices that many farmers and small business people were suffering at the hands of the over powered bankers.

As it transpired Doug Wollerton MP of New Zealand First who knew the Eatwells also felt that a mediation process might be a step in the right direction and he put in a private

Members bill into the ballot also. The difference between the two MP's bills was that Mr Wright had based his bill on the Canadian model, while Mr Woolerton based his on the Australian model.

The Eatwells and other effected people were hopeful that some progress was being made, so on the day the drawing of the private members bill was scheduled Gray and Vickie just happened to be at Parliament, so they were invited to attend the draw from the biscuit tin held in a tiny office hidden in the bowels of the Parliament Buildings. A group of MPs who had bills in the ballot and some junior MPs crowded in and the draw was performed. Just like a meat raffle at the pub Gray reckoned.

As there were two farm debt mediation bills that were much the same a separate draw as to which bill would go into the main draw was carried out and Mr Woolerton's bill won and was in the main draw and luckily it was also drawn to go to the House.

One young MP who had crammed into the tiny room said to Gray with a wry smile, you wouldn't think this is how we run the Country would you. Well that is a mouthful when you know the whole story, he said quietly to Vickie.

Although John Wright was a bit disappointed his bill had not been drawn because he had done a lot of research into the project, but he was still supportive of the ongoing process.

While, the Eatwells were invited to have celebratory drinks with Doug Woolerton and other New Zealand first Members and a few others at the Bellamy's bar at Parliament that evening.

It was a good chance to shoot the breeze with them.

The Parliamentary systems are very slow and tedious at best, but eventually the bill had come up for its first reading in the House and ultimately it was put forward to be debated for its second reading to be heard in the debating chamber of the House of Parliament on 31st March 1999.

They couldn't be in the gallery that day, but the Eatwells did watch most of the debate on Parliament TV.

There was quite a number of MP's that had been supporting the Eatwell's along the way, so they were very hopeful for the bill to progress. Some of the MP's that the Eatwells had approached over the time spoke to the Bill; some were more helpful than others.

It is hard to understand why, but the Federated Farmers were against the Bill and did a lot of lobbying against it, particularly where the Eatwells case was concerned. Maybe there were a few nods and winks between heads of the Federated Farmers and the bankers going on?

The Federated Farmers PR person told the Politicians that the Eatwells had already received mediation when he had been the chairman at one of the meetings at level 22 of the BNZ Building at 1 Willis Street, when to the contrary the Eatwells had a letter from the BNZ clearly stating that the Federated Farmers PR man could act as a chairman only. The banker's letter specified the point that the PR man would not be acting as mediator or arbitrator at the meeting. The Feds man had that a copy of that letter, but still trundled up to Parliament with the Federated Farmers and obfuscated the facts to the politicians in their unexplainable lobby against the Farm Debt Mediation Bill. As far as the Eatwells were aware the Federated Farmers were paying for the PR man's costs.

Why on earth would they do that to their members who are the farmers and a lot of them were being unfairly screwed by their bankers?

They must have been bought off by the money men, or conned by the officials, as it had to be said that something was better than nothing, and nothing was pretty much it for a lot of farmers and small business people with over-zealous bankers chasing their bonuses.

This was the first big lesson into how party politics really dictates the direction of Parliament, because some speakers to the debate had worked with the Eatwells and other victims of banker's pressure, but they were obviously towing the party line far harder than they were pushing the bill through in the debate.

In reality it is only a politically neutral or a populous private Members bill that will get through the House. The Government of the day will always win unless the issue is too contentious or maybe a bill may put pressure on a coalition partner.

John Wright MP spoke to the Farm Debt Mediation Bill, by starting with the courteous *"I would like to congratulate Doug Woolerton on winning not one ballot but two"* He did explain the difference he could see with the Australian model, but he acknowledged that he supported the Woolerton bill and/or he mostly was committed to the fact that the status quo was unacceptable. At least it was one small step in the right direction. In the debate Mr Wright spoke of individual situations he had witnessed, while covering other matters of concern to him saying: *"farmers should not be placed in the position of Mr Eatwell, the farmer from Franz Joseph whose property has been mentioned here tonight, who for months went from the banking ombudsman to the bank, to all other sources, seeking satisfaction. He has a letter from the Banking Ombudsman saying "There are problems here that have not been resolved, but the bank does not appear to want to resolve them". Therefore there is a need to ensure that those people can reach satisfaction. It may not be the sort of satisfaction they want. However, fair play should be what this House is about."*

Owen Jennings MP was one of the MP's who had spent considerable time with the Eatwells, in fact Mr Jennings and his wife had driven all the way to Franz Josef to support them and he also featured in the 60 minutes documentary giving a very sound summary of the situation, but his speech to the House was more about the Act party philosophy, stating:

"The Act party oppose this bill".

No surprises there with the parties connection to the Federated Farmers.

Irrespective of an MP's personal conscience the party will always come first.

Party whips.

Hon Katherine O'Regan was a national party member who had spent quite a lot of time with the Eatwells and spoke to the Bill: *"I rise to speak in this debate because I have an interest in individuals with these problems, which are not entirely to do with debt per se. As a former Minister of Consumer Affairs, I had quite a lot to do with the Banking Ombudsman and its establishment.*

I do not necessarily support the Bill, but I understand the feelings behind it. It should be a lot broader. The House should turn it into an inquiry into banking practice, because the matters that I have been dealing with have led me to see the issue is not so much debt as what happened in the first instance. I think of the Eatwells in particular. In my view if the bank had sat down with them way back 3 years ago, the issues that have arisen ---particularly in the last 12 months and particularly in the last week --- may not have occurred.

The speech went on and in the last paragraph she said: "I hope the select committee will turn its examination into an inquiry into banking practice, and have a very focussed look at how banks deal with clients. It is not necessarily about debt per se', it may be about the way in which a bank manager or a person at a local branch dealt with an individual right at the beginning of the problem".

Prior to the debate when the Bill had a reading slot in the program of the House of Representatives people like John Wright, Katherine O'Regan, Winston Peters and others had said to the Eatwells that the Bill probably won't get through, but it gives us a golden opportunity to get the issues into the

House and might lead at least to some remedial action to be implemented.

Once the debate is recorded on Hansard the statements carry quite high credibility.

High hopes.

Unfortunately the Bill effectively ended there and farm debt mediation was not introduced until 20 years later, but sadly in 1999 the Government of the day simply wiped its hands of it and did nothing of substance after that.

There was a bankers code of practice introduced based on the UK model. The Code is just another smoke screen, because it is set and administered by the bankers and has no powers of enforcement. No systems to help a bank customer with problems.

All other sectors of Industry have laws to ensure fair trading and consumer guarantees, but not the banking industry in New Zealand.

On 30th May 1999 one month after the debate in the House the BNZ sent 15 armed police to the Eatwell farms and the extended family were all evicted under the threat of arrest if they resisted.

The BNZ's dishonest ethics had won.

During the lead up to the Bill being drawn the bankers and their henchmen were trailing up to Parliament in droves to browbeat the politicians into voting against the Bill, which only goes to show that they must have had something to hide as most logical people would see it. If not why would they push back at every attempt to introduce any compliance enforcement of their dodgy business practices?

Why would mediation be such a problem?

One Government Minister told a delegation from the BCAC at Parliament one day that *"you will wait for months get a 30 minute meeting with me, but the bank will take me out to lunch"* He thought that was amusing.

The BCAC delegates didn't see the joke.

It took 20 years until the Farm Debt Mediation Bill was finally passed when Hon Damien O'Connor Minister of Agriculture in the Jacinda Adern Government introduced the Bill as a Government Bill. As the Labour Party was in Government with a healthy majority the Bill was passed pretty much unopposed to all intents and purposes.

Hon Damian O'Connor MP had been involved with the Eatwell case off and on since 1999 and had a good handle on the issues involved. He too gave Gray Eatwell and Jeanette

Walker (a long time lobbyist for struggling farmers) credit for fighting for the Bill for the 20 years it had taken to get there.

Following the passing of the Bill, Gray Eatwell was interviewed by Kate Hawkesby on the early morning show on Newstalk ZB.

(He spoke to other media at the time, but the ZB interview pretty much summed it up).

The brief notes of the Kate Hawkesby interview taken from the ZB web site:

Kate Hawkesby introduced Gray Eatwell:

A much needed helping hand could be on the way to struggling farmers.

With farm debt reaching a record high of $63 billion, the Government's pitching a new mechanism.

It's announced a Farm Debt Mediation Bill, where banks would have to offer farmers mediation, before putting a farm into liquidation or redundancy.

Long-time campaigner for the scheme Gray Eatwell told Kate Hawkesby it's a win-win for banks and farmers.

"If there is a mediation process that's effective and enforceable, then when problems start to arise very early there are often steps to be taken to prevent insolvency and/or manage it."

He says, up until now, they've been outright bullied.

"To be brutally honest, nothing we've seen in these cases would be any different to the worst cases we've seen exposed in the Australian Royal Commission. The practices here are just as bad but they are hidden under the carpet and most people don't realise it is happening."

https://www.newstalkzb.co.nz/on-air/early-edition/audio/gray-eatwell-farmers-say-they-have-been-bullied/?utm_source=share&utm_medium=emai

Now in 2024 discussions with Members of Parliament and news reports are indicative that the bankers are still manipulating farmers in such a way that the high hopes for some relief that would come from mediation has proven to be more of a disadvantage than a remedy, just like the mediation process set up for Sub Post Masters issues in the UK Post Office scandal. In the UK a mediation process was introduced in 2013, but proved to be more of a hindrance than a help and it was abandoned in 2015.

The Bankers are finding ways to use the Farm Debt Mediation Act as a smoke screen, pretty much in the same way the BNZ treated the Banking Ombudsman scheme.

Recently at the UK Inquiry, Alan Bates told the Counsel Jason Beer KC that the mediation system was abused by the Post Office and didn't stop the disgusting prosecutions and gave no tangible relief to the victims.

He told the inquiry he had kept fighting for justice for 23 years so far and that he was concerned that the "Baddies would go scot free", before the inquiry was convened.

The baddies are going "scot free" in New Zealand though.

Not only do they "get off scot free" they are the untouchables in New Zealand business circles.

Mr Bates said there are so many of these big scandals with big firms who need to be held accountable. He knows his stance is right, so he has just dug his heals in until there is proper financial redress for himself and the many other victims of the Post Office's executive brutality and lies.

There have been those persecuted Sub Postmasters who have fallen victim to suicide, but it would be very surprising if any suicides have been committed since Alan Bates started making some progress giving victims some hope for a just outcome.

Accordingly King Charles honour bestowed on Alan Bates is so justified it must be celebrated.

Chapter 8

Petitions to Parliament.

It was recorded in the 2002 Universal Periodic Review Reports of the United Nations Human Rights Council that the New Zealand Government was remiss in its duty to uphold the people's rights to a fair and just hearing by competent Offices of Compliance, with the particular ability to deliver an effective remedy for citizens' complaints, as it is promised under the Universal Declaration of Human Rights.

Therefore improvements were required to be implemented by the New Zealand Government.

From the experience of putting petitions to Parliament in the Eatwell vs Bank of New Zealand case it must be concluded that the Officers of Parliament, including Elected Members simply use industry offices of compliance and commissions as smoke screens in a way that actually obstructs the States International Human Rights obligations and wrongly shifts the responsibility away from themselves, or more importantly from the State.

The industries Offices of Compliance have no powers of enforcement therefore they do not comply with the directive of the United Nations Human Rights Council, i.e. provide effective remedies, and to protect "all people" from oppression.

Commissions such as the Human Rights Commission also fail to comply with the directive because justice must be delivered and enforced to be compliant with International Human Rights law.

Following years of beating on doors seeking a fair hearing, it was on the advice of Dr Nick Smith MP that Mr Eatwell took the first action to petition Parliament with a citizen's petition that was specifically seeking a just hearing for the wrongdoings of the Bank of New Zealand that had been experienced, but unfortunately the Select Committee simply passed the matter back to the Banking Ombudsman who had already been ignored by the Bank and had said loud and clear that there was no more she could do through her office.

It has been demonstrated that as an industry funded smoke screen the Banking Ombudsman scheme has very limited jurisdictional conditions, which renders the office powerless to enforce compliance in any dispute of substance.

Incredibly the Select Committee's Parliamentary offices had been given evidence in correspondence from the Banking Ombudsman stating that her Office could not act in this case, but the situation that followed must be far worse than a simple misunderstanding of the mandate of the Banking Ombudsman scheme.

A copy of a letter that had been provided to the Officials of the Select Committee the Banking Ombudsman Liz Brown stated on 16th May 2002: *"there is nothing in it to change the view I have already expressed to you, which is that there is no further action that can be taken through my office in connection with your concerns about the Bank of New Zealand."*

Petition 2002/47 of Gray Eatwell

The Justice and Electoral Committee has before it the petition of Gray Eatwell requesting that the House inquire into events resulting in the petitioner and his wife being denied natural rights legislated under the New Zealand Bill of Rights Act 1990 and review the legislative restrictions of the Human Rights Commission and the lack of enforcement powers of other consumer and rights based bodies.

Recommendation

We ask that the Banking Ombudsman work in a meaningful manner with Mr Eatwell with a view to resolving his concerns about the actions of a particular banking organisation, and to assist him in addressing the problems he highlights about the processes used by that Office when investigating complaints about banking institutions. We urge the Banking Ombudsman to act promptly in commencing a dialogue with the petitioner.

The reason the Banking Ombudsman was not able to do any more for the Eatwell case was simply due to the recommendations she had made to the Bank were totally ignored. (See John Wright MP speech to the farm debt mediation bill - chapter 7)

In the case of the 2002 petition the Banking Ombudsman Mrs Brown wrote: *"While I was aware that you had presented a petition to Parliament, I was not aware that there had been a Select Committee hearing, nor had I seen a copy of the Select Committee's report. After reading the Select Committee report, I was somewhat concerned at its recommendation, given that I had not been consulted during the hearing process and had not been advised of the*

recommendation made. I therefore sought a meeting with Mr Tim Barnett MP to discuss the report".
In the next paragraph Mrs Brown said" *It became apparent during my discussion with Mr Barnett that he had not seen my letter to you of 16th May 2002 ...."*

There were other letters of evidence given to the Select Committee, but the letter quoted was very clear in its stated position.

That is very confusing because on every occasion a petition was presented to Parliament or a Select Committee had included correspondence from the Banking Ombudsman, because it was her offices inability to provide an effective remedy due to the Bank refusing to accept her recommendations that necessitated the Citizens petition being necessary in the first place, but Tim Barnett indicated to Mrs brown he had not seen the correspondence of the Banking Ombudsman that had been supplied to Parliamentary Officials. This dilemma raises the serious question that there might be something more sinister involved, particularly as it was noted by the Chief Human Rights Commissioner Rosslyn Noonan, within a letter to Hon Peter Dunne MP on the subject: *"If I were a Member of Parliament my query would be whether, in this case, officials had provided fully accurate information on the Human Rights Commission's and the Banking Ombudsman's mandates to the Committees by way of advice on the petitions of Gray Eatwell."*

It was obvious that the Committee was either not given the documents that had been supplied to their officials, or maybe they had not read them, or just dismissed the whole matter in line with the inherent attitude that was emanating around Parliament about the case.

Rosslyn Noonan subsequently wrote to Hon Peter Dunne MP again saying that: *"At the time of Mr Eatwells last petition to Parliament, the Human Rights Commission provided Select Committee with an account of our understanding of the issues of concern to the Eatwells'*

In it we highlighted matters which the Committee may have had regard to. We also made clear a willingness to appear and respond to any questions."

"The frustration for the Eatwells, a frustration I share, was the failure of the Select Committee to acknowledge the limitations on the Human Rights Commission and the Banking Ombudsman, which prevented the Eatwell case being dealt with through either of our processes.

It is rare for the Commission to submit on a private petition to Parliament. We did so in an effort to ensure the Eatwells' were given a fair hearing."

A fair hearing, yeah Right!

They didn't hear the Chief Human Rights Commissioner because the Select Committee didn't even conduct a hearing, which is contrary to what the Prime Minister and the Attorney-General stated.

It is impossible to hold a petition to Parliament hearing when the citizens who are petitioning are not invited to attend. There was a suggestion at one point that there could be a video meeting with the Eatwells, but that didn't happen either.

What actually did happen to give the Officials the idea the petition was closed is a mystery.

Maybe someone in a parliamentary office had got the nod of approval for their home loan.

So we must ask ourselves why the Chief Human Rights Commissioner and the Banking Ombudsman would take so much of their time and effort if they believed there was no substance to the claims being made by the Eatwell's. They had seen the evidence and we heard what Hon Katherine O'Regan MP had told the House of Representatives in the Farm Debt Mediation Bill debate about the same evidence that she had seen and offered advice to the House of the need for it to be investigated further by an official inquiry.

From the discussions with the Parliamentary officials and the stated frustrations expressed by Rosslyn Noonan and Liz Brown it became suspiciously likely that the documents supporting the petition had not been made available on purpose.

Does this mean corruption or incompetence or both?

Either way it is obvious that justice was not going to be delivered without the key evidence being considered by the Select Committee.

Maybe subsequent correspondence from Mr Barnett MP gives another view of the attitude behind this case when he wrote a letter to Mr Eatwell, including office notes clearly not meant for his eyes. Somehow Mr Barnett sent Mr Eatwell some inter office notes and a memo attached to his letter that were clearly written after Liz Brown had been alerted to the Committee recommendations at the meeting with her.   Within the internal memo Mr Barnett, said *"I was approached this week by the Banking Ombudsman. Although her office was at the core of the Select Committee recommendations, they had not been copied with our report and had of course not been consulted during its preparation. The first she knew of the report was when Mr Eatwell wrote to her (we will forward – or you can pick up in my office).*

I think we should copy the petition and our report on it to Liz Brown, the Banking Ombudsman, with a letter acknowledging that she and I meet on the matter subsequent to our report being produced, noting that we had not sought any input from her office prior to the report being produced. We should also urge her to take whatever action is appropriate to further the matter.

We cd copy that to Mr Eatwell, which might shut him up for a while.

We should also copy to her all relevant paperwork, especially any dated since 1/1999

So they weren't actually trying to help the Eatwells get justice, they just wanted him shut up for a while and what could he mean by urging Mrs Brown to take whatever action is appropriate to further the matter. She had said she could do nothing and the bank was ignoring her in any case.

That's on the record.

What Mrs Brown should have done was to ask Parliament why they were making her office look so ineffective through Parliament's dysfunctional systems.

Dysfunction or Corruption by the omission of observing due process?

In person Mrs Brown had expressed her disappointment in Mr Barnett, as she said she had worked with him previously at the Citizens Advice Bureau. She told the Eatwells that she had believed that Mr Barnett was a stickler for justice and she was astounded at his poor performance in his role as Chairman of the Select Committee.

By his inconsistent persona and actions it is most likely Mr Barnett was being influenced from elsewhere, and by the inaccurate responses the Eatwells were receiving from the Prime Minister, Attorney-General and officials it was most likely he was being manipulated from above.

Following this revelation a letter was written to the Prime Minister Helen Clark seeking some explanations as to the attitudes displayed by her party member Tim Barnett. The Prime Minister's reply stated: *"Thank you for your letter concerning the contents of a letter recently sent to you by Tim Barnett MP.*

*I have raised the matter with Mr Barnett. I understand that he met with you in Christchurch recently to discuss your concerns and that he is **pursuing** other avenues by which the Select Committee may be able to investigate your complaint about the Bank of New Zealand.*

I am satisfied that the comment made in the memorandum you received does not reflect the dealings which he and the

Select Committee have had with your case and that there is no sense that your concerns have been dismissed." (The highlighted **pursuing** was the PM's emphasis)

How the Prime Minister could say with any confidence that Mr Barnett's comment does not reflect on the dealings he has had with them, and then imply that he had "discussed their concerns" with the Eatwells when they met in Christchurch is very misleading. The fact is when the Eatwells went to Tim Barnett's Christchurch office they arrived to be met by pleasant PA who was a young man who apologised about Mr Barnett's absence. They chatted for a while, during which, for some obscure reason the PA boasted that he was Tim's partner. They carried on hurrying up to wait for quite some time until Mr Barnett came rushing in saying he was late for another appointment, so after a short discussion the Eatwells were ushered out, feeling very much like they had wasted their time coming all the way to Christchurch.

The actual situation of the meeting certainly didn't rate as the sort of meeting that the Prime Minister seemed to think was in some way helpful in the pursuit of an avenue to progress the Eatwell's citizen's petition and definitely didn't serve justice in any way.

It is hard to reconcile why the Prime Minister might have been motivated to fob the matter off, or play it down, but as there was no further action taken to advance the requested hearing and ultimately the Eatwells definitely felt the sense that their concerns had "been dismissed" because that is what followed.

Another disappointing blind alley of the labyrinth

Justice denied.

Office of the Banking Ombudsman

If any please quote number:

Ref: EB/2866

16 May 2002

Mr Gray Eatwell
226 Sewell Street
HOKITIKA

Dear Mr Eatwell

Thank you for your letter of 8 May 2002.

While I have every sympathy on a personal basis with your situation, and while I have carefully read the enclosures supplied with your letter, there is nothing in it to change the view I have already expressed to you, which is that there is no further action that can be taken through my office in connection with your concerns about the Bank of New Zealand.

Yours sincerely

Liz Brown (Mrs)
Banking Ombudsman

Chapter 9

Peter Dunne/ Lord Arbuthnot.

The fallout from being blocked at every turn was quite wide ranging, and correspondence between various sides of Parliament and the Offices of compliance were flying about, but there was one letter written by Hon Peter Dunne MP addressed to the Chief Human Rights Commissioner Rosslyn Noonan that explains the true position pretty well, while it also demonstrates the Government's determination to shut the case down was either due to Ministers receiving false information and/or was a deliberate betrayal of the States obligations, as a preference to the resultant protection of the BNZ from any forensic scrutiny.

Unfortunately the State was the loser in any event and Human Rights were betrayed.

In Peter Dunne's letter to Rosslyn Noonan he states:

"Gray Eatwell of Invercargill (Gray and Vickie were living in Invercargill for a time working for Real Journeys on their tour boats) *has been in touch with me following your letter to him of 13th July 2006, a copy of which he has kindly provided to me.*

I note with interest your comments at Paragraph 5 that "international human rights law identifies the State as ultimately responsible. While the States responsibilities are largely exercised by the Government of the day, the legislature (Parliament) and the Courts are also key."

"On the basis of these comments, I approached the Attorney General on Mr Eatwells behalf and made the following comments in my letter to him: **"Mr Eatwells dilemma is as follows. On two occasions he has been before a Parliamentary Select Committee and it is clear that on both occasions they have not taken the point that he was making sufficiently seriously. I am not arguing that Mr Eatwells petition has an automatic right to be upheld, but I am a little concerned that as a citizen he has exercised his rights on a number of occasions all to no apparent avail.... In her letter of 13 July 2006 the chief Human Rights Commissioner observes that the Government and the Courts have an equal role in protecting an individual citizen's Human Rights. It is on this basis that I am approaching you as Attorney-General. While Mr Eatwell has been afforded the opportunity of a number of appearances before Select Committees and other institutions, it is questionable whether he has been taken seriously by any of them. He is now left feeling that the entire process is somewhat farcical, and that his rights as a citizen are grossly overstated."**

In his response of 5th September 2006 the Attorney-General Hon Michael Cullen commented:

"I do not agree that Mr Eatwell's situation has not been taken seriously. Two differently constituted Select Committees, the Prime Minister, the Banking Ombudsman and the Human Rights Commissioner have all considered Mr Eatwell's situation. I note also that Mr Eatwell has published a book on the topic and the matter has been before the Courts. On each occasion, Mr Eatwell's situation was considered in some detail. Although this matter has not been resolved to Mr Eatwell's satisfaction, his case has been taken seriously by those considering it. On each occasion, Mr Eatwell was advised either that the person or entity concerned did not have the power to assist him or that, ultimately, there was no legal redress available to him."

The letter continued, Hon Peter Dunne to Chief Human Rights Commissioner Rosslyn Noonan:

"All of which seems to confirm the point of my original approach to the Attorney- General that despite several avenues being pursued Mr Eatwell was effectively being blocked at every turn. That is what brings me back to the comments in your letter regarding the State's role in upholding Human Rights. I note your advice that Mr Eatwell should make a fresh approach to a Select Committee, always

The inaccuracies this letter has highlighted:

The Attorney-General said "Mr Eatwell's situation was considered in some detail".

The question must be what detail?

Most of it was withheld by the officials and the petitioners were not heard. To the contrary those who did have the detail and had heard the petitioner: The Banking Ombudsman, the Chief Human Rights Commissioner and Master Thomas of the High Court Wellington and others, gave very different answers than the Parliamentary processes and political opinions have delivered.

But; it is the legislature that has the obligation of State to uphold International Human Rights Law.

The Human Rights Commissioner advised: "**International Human Rights law identifies the State as ultimately responsible, while the State's responsibilities are largely** *exercised by the Government of the day, the legislature (Parliament) and the Courts are also key."*

One can only ask, how does a citizen make this happen, because if the Courts were "key" then it should not have been possible for the BNZ to override Master Thomas's judgement that the evidence of the Eatwell Livestock Vs BNZ case must be heard and witnesses be cross examined to uphold justice. Furthermore Master Thomas's Judgment was reaffirmed by the Chief Justice Sian Elias by endorsing his judgment as the rule to be followed in any such cases in the future?

If the Courts are "key" to delivering the States obligations to International Human Rights law then obviously the key must have been lost, resulting in a sorry indictment on the Courts and the State.

The fact is that the Court had said for justice to be served the Eatwell case must be heard, but the State through the Attorney-General said the "matter had been before the Courts", when that was a totally misleading statement, because the case had only been before the Court to hear the BNZ's strike out action. The Court ruled against the BNZ, stating that the case must be heard for justice to be delivered, therefore it is very poor form when both the Prime Minister and the Attorney General have made totally inaccurate statements in answer to the reasonable (educated) questions that have been asked by a Member of Parliament.

The Attorney General treated Hon Perter Dunne's correspondence as a party political debate rather than to ensure the truth was provided and to ensure that the States obligations delivered.

Why would he do that?

The Attorney-General says Mr Eatwell has had: "two differently constituted Select Committees, the Prime Minister, the Banking Ombudsman and the Human Rights Commissioner have all considered Mr Eatwells situation"

Maybe that's what he wanted to believe, but the true position is:

The Select Committees made recommendations that the case should go to the Banking Ombudsman, but the Banking Ombudsman had made it very clear that this was not possible:

In a letter that had been supplied to the Select Committee sent on 16 May 2002, Liz Brown the Banking Ombudsman wrote: "…..I have expressed to you, there is no further action that can be taken through my office in connection with your concerns about the Bank of New Zealand."

Even with the letter being supplied to the Parliamentary staff the Select Committee report stated:

Recommendation:

We ask that the Banking Ombudsman work in a meaningful manner with Mr Eatwell with a view to resolving his concerns about actions of a particular banking organisation…………………………"

Then:

The Banking Ombudsman wrote: 2nd June 2004 re second petition:

"After reading the Select Committee report, I was somewhat concerned at its recommendation, given I had not been consulted during the hearing process and had not been advised of the recommendation made. I therefore sought a meeting with Tim Barnett MP…" The letter went on *"It became apparent during my discussions with Mr Barnett that he had not seen my letter to you of 16 May 2002……….."*

Fancy that: Tim Barnett was the chairman of the Justice and Electoral Committee and it appears that he hadn't seen Mrs Browns letter.

But the Chief Human Rights Commissioner had also observed:

"If I were a Member of Parliament my query would be whether, in this case, officials had provided fully accurate information on the Human Rights Commissions and the Banking Ombudsman's mandates to the committees by way of advice on the petitions of Gray Eatwell."

So:

The Chief Human Rights Commissioner thinks someone in the official Parliamentary office of the Committee had not provided the "fully accurate information" to the Select Committee.

Next:

In a letter to the Speaker of the House Hon Lockwood Smith MP the question was put by Mr Eatwell: "I am seeking your advice on what course of redress is available to a citizen when their fundamental Human Rights are obstructed by failures in the Parliamentary process".

The Speaker replied: *"If a Committee considers that it has been misled or obstructed then any member of the committee is able to raise a matter of Parliamentary privilege with the Speaker."*

Well stone the crows: Not one member of the committee did that.

Why not?

The committee was made aware that critical, "fully accurate information" had not been considered by them, (as it appears) thus making an absolute mockery of their recommendation. But they ignored that fact.

So if the members of a Select Committee fail to take remedial actions when they have been advised they have been "mislead or obstructed", while carrying out their duties as a member appointed to a Select Committee, what course of redress is available to a petitioning citizen to ensure the States obligations are met?

But then after all this:

The Prime Minister Helen Clark wrote : "I am advised that Tim Barnett did all in his power to help you, and working with Hon Peter Dunne, helped to ensure that two separate Select Committees heard your case…………."

Are you serious Prime Minister?

You said that "Tim Barnett did all in his power to help you". He was the Chairman of the Committee and he didn't even act on the the matter of the breach of Parliamentary privilege.

Whoever had "misled or obstructed" the Select Committee were obviously in breach of Parliamentary privilege.

But the Parliamentary Officials said that the petition had been heard and nothing more could be done, without giving any consideration to the fact that it was the officials who Rosslyn Noonan believes had failed to supply the evidence to the Committee.

It is rather suspicious that the officials said that the Petition was closed when the petitioners hadn't even been heard.

So did the tail wag the dog, or had the Committee failed in its obligations?

Whatever transpired the result is that the State had breached its obligations under the International Human Rights laws, again.

It is quite unnerving to realize that the Prime Minister Helen Clark and the Attorney-General Michael Cullen, must have been given a completely inaccurate summary of the facts, which by its content has emphasised the shambles that the Parliamentary systems have become.

Were the heads of Government given inaccurate information on which they made the ultra vires explanations they did, or were the leaders supporting a preconceived whitewash?

If the Prime Minister knew that the Select Committee had not received the crucial documents they needed, she could surely not have supported Tim Barnett's stated performance, so why didn't the Prime Minister know the truth?

Or did she?

Tim Barnett as chairman of the Select Committee had written several letters and in one such bundle of correspondence he had accidently included an incriminating internal memo that said *"We could copy that to Mr Eatwell, which might shut him up for a while."*

So:

If the Prime Minister's opinion was that *"Mr Barnett did all in his power to help you"* that certainly did not provide the required level of governance that could deliver the States ultimate responsibility to uphold International Human Rights law.

The Chief Human Rights Commissioner had said *"At the time of Mr Eatwell's last petition to Parliament, the Human Rights Commission provided the Select Committee with an account of our understanding of the issues of concern to the Eatwells'*

In it we highlighted matters which the Committee may have had regard to. We also made clear a willingness to appear and respond to any questions."

But of course Rosslyn Noonan has said that the officials had not provided "fully accurate information" to the Select Committee anyway.

And she wasn't invited to "respond to any questions" either.

The Chief Human Rights Commissioner had also said that she shared Mr Eatwells frustration;

No surprises there.

Whatever next:

It is blatantly clear by now that the whole parliamentary process is nothing short of a shambles, when even the Parliamentary officer Alex Botar wrote to Hon Peter Dunne saying "The Banking Ombudsman may still find in favour of Mr Eatwell...."

To which:

The Banking Ombudsman, who by now was also getting very frustrated at being ignored and being used as a scapegoat up at Parliament, because she wrote directly to:

Alex Botar (Himself)
Parliamentary Officer
Office of the Clerk of the
House of Representatives
Parliament
Wellington.

And so, in the very proper way that Mrs Brown always conducted herself and spoke, she said: *"the Hon Peter Dunne has asked me to confirm to you that there is no possibility of progressing his (Eatwell) complaint through the Banking Ombudsman process."*

Remembering that it was said by the Attorney-General that two Select Committees, the Prime Minister, the Banking Ombudsman, and the Human Rights Commissioner have all considered Mr Eatwell's situation"

The Attorney-General missed out the Wirth Circus in his reply because that is what it was like.

Mind you, if Wirths Circus was as clumsy as Parliament is there would have been a lot of trapeze artists falling off their swings, and lion tamers losing limbs and getting eaten.

Although the above Parliamentary circus may seem like a comedy of errors to you, it is hard not to consider what would have happened if the Eatwells' had not been fighting the BNZ and that they didn't have the proof the bank had broken the law? (See Hon Pete Hodgson reply to Question in the House of Representatives - chapter 10)

 And why would the officials withhold crucial documents from the Select Committee?

Simply put, the parliamentary systems were proven to be totally dysfunctional in this matter and Justice was the victim.

What was the motivation for the shocking performance of the Parliamentary process and how much say did the BNZ and/or their henchmen/lobbyists have in all of this?

Did they threaten the Government with the potential of the bank collapsing, if an official investigation was invoked, and the Government was scared of the impact on the economy that could follow and that would not be good for them at the next election?

If the Eatwell case was not valid, ask the question as to why all of the qualified people and official offices, that had received evidence of the banks wrongdoing, didn't question the validity of the case?

The case has been seen by many and discredited by none.

Arithmetic does not lie and the coincidence between the Irish Bank and the BNZ cannot be ignored.

Maybe the heads of Government did know what was going on with the Irish High Court investigation of the Irish bank and they didn't want to risk the same potential disruption to the New Zealand banking industry.

In the early stages of the Irish High Court investigation there was quite a rumbling of concern about the potential for a serious banking industry breakdown in Ireland and beyond.

It is actually very hard to believe that the Government weren't advised through International protocols about an issue as big as the National Irish Bank case and the possible damage that could impact on a major bank with considerable investment in New Zealand.

It is on the record that the Reserve Bank was advised by the Irish High Court.

Money power first and Justice a distant last again.

At one stage the Prime Minister had said in a letter discussing Tim Barnett's stupid memo Faux Par when she assured Gray and Vickie Eatwell "…..that there is no sense that your concerns have been dismissed."

In contradiction the Banking Ombudsman and the Chief Human Rights Commissioner had followed up for a long time of frustration, simply because they had seen too much of the truth and had enough integrity not to ignore it, but unfortunately the systems they worked with had exposed its own weakness which had reduced them to being toothless Tigers. Lizzy Brown detested the thought that she may be seen as a toothless Tiger, but sadly for all her efforts that is what she was exposed as being.

Obviously Liz Brown and Rosslyn Noonan had a higher standard of personal integrity that exceeded their powers of enforcement of their respective offices mandate. (Or at least the publically perceived mandate)

Ministry of Justice information states:

"Parliament gives no power to decide unfairly and therefore by doing so the decision maker exceeds his powers. His decision is therefore Ultra Vires and outside his jurisdiction. Similarly, if a decision is unreasonable in the relevant sense it is Ultra Vires and in excess of or outside the decision makers jurisdiction".

The ill-founded hallowed Select Committee recommendation given was obviously Ultra Vires because it was seriously inadequate due to the absence of the evidence that could not be considered, which could be due to the failure of the

Parliamentary processes. In effect the anomalies had engineered the Select Committee into the impossible situation of not being able to provide a fair decision in the Eatwell petition; therefore the subsequent Government advice based on it must also be Ultra Vires.

Butterworths Law Dictionary-Ultra Vires: (Latin: Beyond the power) an ultra vires act is beyond the legal power or authority of a person, institution or legislation, and therefore invalid.

According to the obvious considered and/or recklessly perceived intention to shut the Eatwells case down it is very hard not to think of corruption particularly when the Bank of New Zealand's track record is considered, but the most disturbing fact to emerge is that the State of New Zealand is failing all New Zealanders by its inability to uphold International Human Rights law to its citizens particularly when there is a foreign owned corporate involved.

The Attorney- General mentioned the Eatwells case has been before the Courts, which of course is true, but what he didn't want to admit to Peter Dunne, or didn't know, was the fact that the High Court's Master Thomas made his judgment in the Eatwells favour. It was a judgment that focused on the high principle of the right to a just hearing where the Master emphasised the fact that the evidence must be heard and witnesses cross examined for that justice to be served.

This renders the Attorney- General's answer as being ultra vires because it was totally wrong and grossly unfair.

The High Court judgment in Eatwell Livestock vs Bank of New Zealand has been elevated by the Chief Justice in the rules followed by the Court, to be the Master Thomas's principle to be followed when a strike out action is heard.

The fact is that the High Court was subsequently treated with blatant contempt by overriding the judgment's ruling; by deliberately misleading another Court's Master into bankrupting the Eatwells and then following up by ensuring that the Official Assignee filed to discontinue the Eatwell claim in the Court, without the authority to do so.

The result is that the high bar of justice set by Master Thomas has been corrupted irrespective of the fact that every effort had been made to request the Government to correct the injustice.

Mr Eatwell considered taking the case to the United Nations Justice Committee to which the Chief Human Rights Commissioner had offered her assistance, but by this time Gray Eatwell was totally worn down physically, financially, emotionally and mentally, so he just didn't have the strength to follow through to the UN at the time.

Subsequently, Rosslyn Noonan was promoted to be a member of the United Nations Justice Committee and could have been a big help in showing the way.

Maybe she still will.

It would be quite easy to prove that the New Zealand Government is failing in its obligations to the International body, by demonstrating the inability to ensure the legislature can operate efficiently enough to uphold the high standard of its responsibilities to the State.

In view of the fact that the Legislature upholds the States obligations to the international Human Rights Laws, it is interesting that in 2001 under the letter head including the Leader of the House of Representatives the Minister stated that, *"I understand that you and your associates believe that a Bank can take actions against a client that may, for example financially disadvantage or bankrupt that client. If the remedy is to sue the Bank, the remedy is defective because the action of the Bank itself has reduced the capacity of the client to take advantage of the remedies available- the client has no money and can't afford to sue. That may be a reasonable grievance, ..."*

Does the Minister mean a Bank can steal a client's money and then bankrupt them so they can't afford to sue? Well that is exactly what the BNZ has done to the Eatwell family and many others.

As the Leader of the House of Representatives the Minister must hold the mandate to ensure that the legislature is upholding its responsibility to the State, therefore for the Minister to respond to Mr Eatwell by offering an impossible course of action when as a citizen he was simply seeking the right to justice as promised by the State, the decision the Minister gave has exceeded his powers and would also be rendered as being Ultra Vires.

The constant inconsistencies of the answers given by the heads of State and other Elected Members and officials are indicative of the intention was to obfuscate the facts.

Lord James Abuthnot MP UK was so horrified at learning what the UK Post Office had done to innocent sub Postmasters that he stuck his neck out and did a lot of work to help Alan Bates and the sub Postmasters group expose the truth. Very much like it is demonstrated in this chain of correspondence showing the amount of effort Hon Peter Dunne MP (NZ) invested to see justice for the Eatwells. Accordingly it has been very interesting watching the current official inquiry into the UK Post Office scandal to see emails between the executives in the evidence discussing how they could deal with Lord Abuthnot's snooping eyes. It is most likely there were similar emails being shared about Perter

Dunne and the other good members of the New Zealand Parliament who could see the injustice that had been served to the Eatwell family and other victims of the out of control New Zealand Banking Industry.

Chapter 10

The question to the House:

Following the Eatwell's meeting with the Ex-Prime Minister at Parliament there was some more correspondence from Mrs Shipley where in one letter she said *"I personally still believe that a well-focused Select Committee Inquiry may well be the best way to bring out the issues which are of real concern to you, to have some of them investigated and, at least for the future, put procedures in place which will avoid the experience you have been exposed to."*

But of course this was blocked at every turn, but with the experience of how Select Committees can get manoeuvred it is not likely that this process could cope with finding a sound resolution with all the complexities and the smoke and mirrors that are systemic within the banking practices.

The big business and the bankers lobby is very powerful up at Parliament, but to add insult to injury it was reported in the news media recently that they have even given the big time lobbyists swipe cards to get into parliament without going through security .

Funnily enough, Gray Eatwell ran in 3 General Elections and always said all he really wanted was a swipe card so he couldn't keep getting locked out.

Every level of Government knew exactly the foundation of the pleadings of the Eatwells that were being trumpeted all around the Parliament buildings, but to get any action was impossible.

Gordon Copeland MP was one of many Members of Parliament to assist the Eatwells in their plight to be delivered a just hearing . Mr Copeland wrote several letters to Cabinet Ministers and Officials and he put it to them as to why was Mr Eatwell getting nothing but "lame duck excuses" in his efforts to be heard.

This direct approach did get some sparks flying and/or hands wringing.

The Eatwells approached many MPs over the years, but of all the Members they met from all sides of the House Gordon Copeland was a man with the highest of moral principles. His integrity was such that he eventually put his political career on the line over a matter with moral implications that he opposed based on his personal morals. The problem of making this stand was that he was at odds with his party, so he decided to resign rather than vote against his moral principles.

This action was effectively the end of his time as a Member of Parliament other than the run up to the next election during which time he acted as an independent MP.

Gordon Copeland was known for being a very cautious and thorough person, so he definitely would not have been prepared to support the Eatwell case as strongly as he did if he was not confident in the honesty of the Eatwells and the integrity of their case.

There were quite a number of other Members who supported the Eatwells to the point of being their towering strength during some very low periods, but unfortunately even the most valued

supporting MP's would melt away under the power of the Party whip. They were never expected to cross the floor, but there was always the hope they might convince their party to support them to bring that elusive remedy.

Sadly even with the evidence the MP's had, the Bankers lobby was too strong for them.

Following a considerable period of duck shoving and diversions Gordon Copeland decided to lodge a question to the Minister of Commerce in the House of Representatives, as follows:

The New Zealand House of Parliament Hansard report: 14 July 2007 oral question to the Minister of Commerce Hon Pete Hodgson.

7. GORDON COPELAND (United Future) to the **Minister of Commerce**: Is he confident that the interest-charging procedures of banks operating in New Zealand are subject to adequate legal scrutiny?

Hon PETE HODGSON (Minister of Commerce): Mostly.

Gordon Copeland: Is the Minister aware that Gray Eatwell and the Bank Customer Action Collective have made numerous efforts to have the interest-charging procedures of the Bank of New Zealand investigated by various authorities, including the Serious Fraud Office, the Commerce Commission, the Banking Ombudsman, and the Minister of Finance, yet, to date, a full investigation has not been undertaken; and does he think that is acceptable?

Hon PETE HODGSON: Yes, I am aware of the gentleman's activity over many years, and I am aware of his group. I am also aware that the authorities that he has approached have pretty well universally come to the view that he does not have prima facie evidence apart from that in his own case, in which the Bank of New Zealand overcharged him and then refunded him about $20,000.

Gordon Copeland: Is the Minister aware of an overseas court finding that the National Irish Bank has been engaged in illegal interest overcharging, and given the fact that the National Australia Bank was the parent company of the National Irish Bank at the time, and is still the parent company of the Bank of New Zealand, has he considered whether the New Zealand authorities are giving this matter the amount of attention it properly deserves?

Hon PETE HODGSON: The answer to the first question is yes. The answer to the second question is that as soon as they are presented with sufficient prima facie evidence I would be confident that they would act.

Gordon Copeland: Will the Minister consider appointing a suitable forensic accountant to conduct a preliminary investigation into this matter, so that the facts can be established and justice finally delivered to the Bank Customers Action Collective after its 10-year fight; if not, why not?

Hon PETE HODGSON: No, we already have investigative and enforcement agencies, in the form of the Commerce Commission or, if there is fraudulent activity, the Serious Fraud Office, and it is to those bodies, which are independent of the Crown, that Mr Eatwell or anyone else should turn.

Butterworths Law Dictionary:

Prima facie evidence: Evidence which establishes prima facie case in favour of the party adducing it.

In criminal cases, prima facie evidence is sufficiency of evidence upon which a person could be convicted of an offence. [EVIDENCE]

Therefore Minister Pete Hodgson's answer is saying that the gentleman's evidence is of sufficiency to convict the BNZ of an offense

The reactions to the Minister's answers:

The fact is that the SFO (and others) were supplied with bank statement documents that changed in their format when the overcharges were applied in a way that human intervention had to be applied to achieve this result. It was not possible for a computer system to cause this result to occure. The Irish High Court Investigators report detailed the process used in Ireland to hide the interest loadings that also required the same human intervention by altering the figures.

It seems as if the claims that Parliament stands for justice in reality is a lie because there is never an accessible right of reply possible for the common person, however if given the right to reply in this case it would have been along these lines:

But, Minister Pete Hodgson; within the second question you were told that Mr Eatwell and others have already been to the so called investigative agencies you have noted. Therefore the Minister's answer is an unreasonable response, because it is due to the failure of the named agencies to act that has led to the question being necessary, and by its inference is an indictment on Parliament's obligations to provide the rule of law to all people.

It is said that the agencies you have noted are independent of the Crown, but isn't there an obligation for the Crown to uphold International Human Rights law? That is what is being pleaded.

The Minister claimed to be aware of the Irish High Court case, but he clearly hadn't understood it very well, because if he did he would know that in Ireland the overcharging practice wasn't detected by the customers of the bank. It was too well hidden. It was a NIB bank manager with a guilty conscience who spilled the beans to RTE and it was the inspectors who found the volume of the practice involved. So why did Minister Pete Hodgson put the onus on Mr Eatwell or anyone else to go back to the "enforcement agencies" that he already knew had ignored them on every occasion before.

That was the whole purpose of the question!

(An interesting fact is that the Irish investigators found that the average amount taken from the Irish banks customers was a far lower amount than the BNZ had been caught taking.)

Accordingly, the Minister's answer given to the House of Representatives actually exacerbated the facts and magnified the frustration of justice denial being imposed by the elaborate cover-up that has been applied.

This official exchange in the House of Parliament on 14th July 2007 comes after years of correspondence with all levels of Government and its offices of authority proving categorically that the New Zealand Government have been made fully aware of the evidence of overcharging by the BNZ, to which the Minister admits there is prima facie evidence, therefore the failure to act must constitute an abdication of the State's duty to protect the public from white collar crime of the complexity that has been exposed in this case.

The New Zealand Government should be warned that as the Irish Director of Corporate Enforcement Paul Appleby had warned the Irish people when his report was released that a failure to arrest "white collar crime" would lead to "social disruption and economic damage".

The human and financial damage caused to many good families in New Zealand as identified in the book "You can Bank of it", details how the failure to prosecute the actions of the BNZ has definitely resulted in "significant social disruption" and far reaching "economic damage" to New Zealand and the unprotected bank customers involved.

The Minister stated to the House that he was aware that Gray Eatwell has produced prima facie evidence in his own case, in which the Bank of New Zealand overcharged him about $20,000, but the Minister totally ignored the fact that such an action in itself was evidence that the BNZ had committed a crime; which was the same act as the National Irish Bank had done. He implied that because the BNZ had refunded about $20,000 (which is totally inaccurate) that in doing so, justice had in some way been served.

It would be interesting to know how the Minister came up with the $20,000 figure, because it sounds just like the BNZ's flippant statement that has been bandied about elsewhere by the bankers.

(The actual figure has never been refunded).

There is prima facie evidence that proves a Bank had deliberately stolen a customer's money, but is the Minister suggesting to the House that this customer had been singled out to be the only customer to be robbed in this sinister way?

Clearly the Minister and many others who have formed their uneducated opinion on this crime have no idea how hard it is to detect the fact that the Bank is loading up interest and other fees on your account. Even many of the Bankers couldn't get it right when they were required to quantify the accurate amounts involved and several accountants had signed off bank statements without noticing the overcharges.

The fact is that the Eatwells only stumbled onto the excesses when in one month the Bank had increased the interest charge on one working account by a much larger amount than the month before. It was not that easy for them to notice because the Eatwells were at their peak in the Fishing Industry during the heady days in the late 1980's when bank interest rates for over drafts went above 20%, so high interest charges were not uncommon for them to see.

They had done a major rebuild on the Fishing Trawler Cook Canyon in 1987 that had cost them over $1.1m and had traded with quite large swings in income and expenditure that meant that their bank accounts fluctuated in pretty large lumps quite often.

So when the excess was noticed they simply thought it was an error and the bank would fix it. They didn't, and although the Minister said the Bank had only pinched $20,000 and given it back he actually was in cloud cuckoo land because the bank only acknowledged the theft after years of complaining and many attempts to get the Eatwells to agree that various low figure estimates would make up a full and final figure.

Their figures were not accurate so could not be full and/or final.

The problem was that when the Bank refused to rectify the problem and/or tried horse trading ; in order to resolve the matter accurately the Eatwells set about reconstructing there bank statements from the date they had shifted their banking to the BNZ.

The reason people don't notice they have been ripped off is that with a trading overdraft account every single days balance has to be calculated at the correct interest rate for one day and then apply it to the account at the end of every month, on the same day that the statement shows the interest figure being applied.

A busy working account can go into credit one day and debt the next and back to credit within days, so to be precise extreme care is required.

The account that the overcharges were first noticed the account was actually in credit during that particular month.

This sounds easy, but it's not.

The key trick that is frequently overlooked is that the loan documents specify the interest rate and penalty rates that can be charged for various reasons; (unfortunately a lot of people have lost these important documents) however it has been found that when an account is under stress the penalty rate charged often exceeds the documented rate. I.e. penalties are applied at higher rates than the official contract documents specify.

Banks will justify this practice by making the excuse of risk increase to the bank, but unfortunately any excess to the contracted rate is illegal, and the bank had in most situations created the increased risk themselves anyhow.

There is no way that the Eatwells case is an isolated case as the Minister seemed to have been implying to the House, but unfortunately the true figures will never be known because the authorities failed in their duty to investigate the complaint to which the said prima facie evidence had proved that there was a very complex crime to be investigated.

"The baddies got off scot free".

Isolating people who report errors in the system is being accepted as a common corporate practice globally.

At the UK Post Office scandal inquiry it has been said how the Post Office executive's tactic was to tell the sub Postmasters who complained that the IT system was faulty, by telling them that they were the only person to report the problem and continued to accuse them of theft.

Minister Hon Pete Hodgson MP must have been an apologist of this behaviour to excuse the same tactic being applied in New Zealand.

Villainise the person to camouflage the crime.

That would surely be an even greater crime, but the answer demonstrated that the Minister had no intention of upholding the law in this case. He had admitted there was prima facie evidence of theft but, "no not me Guv".

The State was betrayed again.

To recap, the first supplementary question put by Gordon Copeland said that Gray Eatwell had made numerous efforts to have interest-charging procedures of the Bank of New Zealand investigated by various authorities, including the Serious Fraud Office, the Commerce Commission, the Banking Ombudsman, and the Minister of Finance, yet to date a full investigation has not been undertaken: The Minister totally ignored the detail of the question when he replied *"No. We already have investigative and enforcement agencies, in the form of the Commerce Commission, if there is fraudulent activity, the Serious Fraud Office"*,

The Minister stated in the House of Representatives that he was aware of the "gentleman's" (Gray Eatwell's) activity over many years and that he is aware that he has prima facie evidence of overcharging by the BNZ, which is a mirror of the same revelation that invoked the Irish High Court investigation that adjudged that the practice applied by the NIB was a serious crime. By comparison, Mr Eatwell discovered a practice of the BNZ that has produced exactly the same result as the Irish Inspectors have, excepting the point that the amounts of money taken from the Eatwell accounts was far greater than the average figure discovered by the Irish High Court.

The Minister stated that he was aware of the Irish High Court investigation into the National Irish Bank; however he must have overlooked how the overcharging practice was identified in Ireland. The High Court report makes it clear that the practice was very difficult to identify due to the method used to hide the overcharges.

The magnitude of the overcharges was identified by the High Court inspectors, not the Irish bank's customers.

It is unacceptable that the legislature will wittingly ignore prima facie evidence of a crime that has been hidden by a New Zealand registered bank, particularly under the circumstances it was discovered and the extreme measures the BNZ took to cover up the crime must ring warning bells in the offices of authority commissioned with the statutory mandate of compliance enforcement in New Zealand.

In her letter 13th March 2002 following the meeting at her office Mrs Shipley had said *"I personally believe that a well-focused Select Committee Inquiry may well be the best way to bring out the issues which are of real concern to you, to have some of them investigated and, at least for the future, put procedures in place which will avoid the experience you have been exposed to."* That was the person who had apologised for getting it wrong on the National Party's "watch".

Unfortunately Hon Pete Hodgson had pretty much told the House of Parliament that the "well-focused Select Committee inquiry" recommended by ex-Prime Minister Jenny Shipley, the Chief Human Rights Commissioner Rosslyn Noonan, Hon Katherine O'Regan and others, was not going to be delivered on his "watch".

It is hard to reconcile how a Minister of the Crown can live with their conscience when they make ministerial statements, as it was in this instance, Hon Pete Hodgson had effectively told the House that in his assessment of the situation that it was OK that the BNZ had stolen about $20,000 (not accurate) but had given it back.

In view of this mind-set the Minister had blithely made this judgment to bat Gordon Copeland's question off, when he acknowledged the fact that the Eatwells had been battling with the BNZ for years trying to have the overcharging practice remedied. In effect the Minister has indicated that he is happy to accept the fact that the BNZ had bankrupted the Eatwells with the sole purpose to intercept the High Court hearing the facts of the case that would expose the unlawful practices of the bank.

During the years leading up to Gordon Copeland taking his question to the House the case had been taken to every office of authority in New Zealand including the Serious Fraud Office who fobbed the Eatwells off telling them to get more evidence, even though they had been given prima facie evidence of the illegal overcharges.

There has been much written about the SFO over the years including criticism of the founding director Charles Sturt, but it was interesting to learn from him that in the first four and half years of the SFO's existence that 18 of 41 prosecutions were cases where no complaints from the victims received and in many instances people had been completely unaware that they had been defrauded. Charles Sturt claimed that the success of the office "was due to a proactive policy that had contributed significantly to the true worth of the SFO differing from similar agencies in the Western world."

Somewhere the SFO must have lost their way.

Chapter 11

MP's and Celebrities coerced.

As the finance companies were tipping up in 2008 losing good people's retirement funds by the billions it was disgusting to find how many big named ex PM's such as ex-Prime Minister Jim Bulger and there was Wyatt Creech (ex-Deputy Prime Minister) and John Luxton who were enticed by Mark Bryers to sit on the Board of Blue Chip. They resigned as directors when the heat came on and they could see that they had been supporting a scam, but unfortunately the damage was already done because thousands of good people had been sucked in to entrust their money to the Blue Chip scheme. Many of them invested their money because they felt safe with these well-known people on the board of directors.

They actually were financially literate and had done their homework (or thought they had).

Sir Douglas Graham another ex-cabinet minister and Hon William Jeffries ex- Labour Party MP and other well-known individuals were courted by finance companies to be directors on their boards, because the high flying people setting up finance companies were well aware of the value to prospective investors it would be to see such respected names on the board of directors and just like the Blue Chip example they felt safe to invest their money with them. The promoters would make a point of telling prospective investors the known people they had on the board as an enticement to convince them how secure the company was.

High flying people like Eric Watson also gave people false trust in the investment companies they were running.

Even my old friends Sir Colin and Lady Verna Meads were enticed into doing a promotion for Provincial Finance that went down the gurgler with the others. The Meads read the script and fronted a TV commercial that made it look like they were happy customers, but in reality the Meads had been broken by the BNZ and were simply using Colin's massive celebrity status to make some much needed income and of course the finance company grabbed them with glee.

What a coup that was.

It's amazing to compare the attitude of the Finance companies towards the value of fame, when on the other side we see that the BNZ were justifying their actions of taking the Meads down by saying he was "a good rugby player, but a hopeless business man".

It boggles the mind to see how they got away with discrediting Colin to cover up their own crimes, while they were slandering him at the same time that Colin was announced as New Zealand's rugby player of the century.

Sadly, it goes to show how our fellow New Zealanders behave when a person experiences financial problems, because as much as the mighty Pine Tree was loved and respected in New Zealand, the old Chinese whispers that he was broke went around. The Bankers saying he was "a great rugby player, but a hopeless business man" sat quite comfortably with far too many people who were quite happy to go along with the old Kiwi adage "I'm right Jack" when money is involved.

Some people just didn't want to accept that the great man had been scammed and he didn't like talking about it. That is why he supported Wallace Connell and Gray Eatwell to speak for him about how the BNZ had bought them down with a dodgy loan deal.

Colin and Verna had told Gray and Vickie Eatwell the same thing they had told Brian Turner when he was writing the book "Meads".

They explained how they had borrowed money from over-seas (or so they thought) via the bank (BNZ) but it turned into a nightmare that caused a battle with the bank that had lasted for many years.

When it all went pear shaped they had discovered one morning that they owed the bank half a million more than they thought they did.

They never recovered from the losses they had suffered.

When the Eatwells first met Colin and Verna they said how very dejected, angry and despairing they were. At that time Verna was fighting cancer that she firmly believed was induced by the stress of the loss of their land and the long dispute with the bank.

No arguments there.

Just another big corporate "trampling on unprotected people".

Wallace Connell meticulously reconstructed the trail of the bogus loan scheme that showed how some of the over-seas loans can't have been taken out, but the Bank just raked in the money from all the charges and exchange rate movements etc.

Sadly it is too late to prove how sinister the practice was, but individuals like Colin and Verna never recovered, in more ways than one, from the total lack of law enforcement they had witnessed.

As it is said in "You can Bank on it" all they wanted was "justice no more no less".

With no compliance enforcement available in New Zealand, the corporate crooks got away with it, and the Meads and their many colleagues just had to live with it.

Mind you at a later time, the BNZ ran an advertisement on TV for a while that showed a photo of one of Colin's rugby jerseys within the clip. The BCAC made such a fuss to the rugby union and the TV station about the insult to the Meads that the advertisement was removed pretty quickly.

The bankers seemed to have forgotten that it was their wonderful scheme that had been sold to selected customers including the Meads by convincing them that their business would gain considerably by signing up for the overseas loans they were promoting. The bank took securities over the customer's assets when signing them up and when the scheme hit the wall (as it was always going to) the banks foreclosed on those assets and sold the customer's business down the river, leaving the hard working business owners broke and emotionally trashed.

Wallace Connell was one of the business men, who had taken on the foreign loans that were sold to him by the same bankers, and he too had also been driven to ruin when the so called foreign currency loans fell over so he undertook the massive amount of work to unpick the details of the off shore loan scheme to see what went wrong and why. His massive spread sheet demonstrated that the loans were a fabrication that was primarily structured to boost the bank's profit line, while offering the customers little more than high costs and unreasonable levels of risk that had been clouded from their view.

Gray Eatwell and others were shown Wallace's work, which in this day and age of computers might seem ridiculous, but his accuracy and precision plotting the trail of transactions was incontrovertible, but amazingly the authorities refused to act on it.

The issue of the bogus foreign currency loans (became known as forex) was raised in the Farm Debt Mediation Bill debate in the House of Representatives in John Wright MP's speech when he said: *"We are not talking about an equal contest. One is a large corporate with ongoing resources to fight legal battles through the Courts. The other is a person under some financial stress"* (created by the Bank) *"who has no recourse, very often, to the Courts, simply because he or she cannot afford it financially. A group of Bank of New Zealand customers were involved in what became known as the foreign currency loans affair, some of whom are still seeking redress through the Courts and trying to square things up with the Bank of New Zealand over events that happened in the late 1980's."*

The Irish High Court report indicates that the detail of how this scheme was set up is not a lot unlike the CMI product that was found to be illegal in Ireland, but in the absence of comparable law enforcement in New Zealand it will never be known.

Mr Connell formed the group Mr Wright noted in the House that was made up of victims of the off shore loans that were eventually declared to be a scam, with the objective to push for an official investigation into the practices that had impacted on their businesses and ultimately they hoped for restitution, no differently than the group Alan Bates had set up in the UK.

Colin and Verna Meads were part of that group and attended nearly all of the meetings that were called to discuss how a just result could be found. They travelled quite a distance to the meetings with the hope of restitution for their losses, because they knew the bank's actions that had been enforced on them were not acceptable under any business standards.

At the end, Sir Colin Meads grimly hung on to his life as he battled cancer waiting for the unveiling of the brass monument that was being skilfully sculptured of him as the formidable rugby player that he was as a younger man.

It was quite emotional to see the frail old man Colin had become at the ceremony on Te Kuiti's main street outside the railway station at the unveiling ceremony.

But he had made it just like the tough old bloke he had always been.

The great man was so graciously humble that day; He loved the detail of the brass statue saying *"he (the artist) even got my boot laces just how I tied them"*. But sadly Colin only survived for another 2 months following that day. *May he rest in peace.*

As it is printed in the book "You can Bank on it" which has a photo featuring Colin Meads on the back cover, with the preface to the book included the parts of a discussion held with Gray and Vickie Eatwell in the Meads kitchen:

"The mighty "Pine Tree" Meads, who is a victim of his bungling bankers, the old rugby lock said as he waved his big strong fist about his bulky frame:

"They bully you – they badger you – Their stand-over tactics are overpowering-

There is no justice in New Zealand –

But, all I want is to see justice, no more, no less".

Justice never came for Sir Colin and Lady Verna and the other people who had been scammed by their bank with the bogus foreign currency loans, and there was no official investigation, no restitution and no justice for the great man and the many other good people who had much of their lives destroyed by the greedy banker's dodgy scheme they signed up to trusting their bankers assurances.

SIR COLIN MEADS
ALL BLACK
1957-1971
New Zealand's Player
of the 20th Century

When the banks went about discrediting the affected customers with the intention to hide their own dishonesty they conveniently forgot all the enticements they had expounded when they sold to people like the Meads and the others that were tricked into taking up the bogus loans. Irrespective of all the flash promises they made to convince them that they would be so much better off. However in the ultimate collapse the Bankers had no compunction in foreclosing on those good people's assets when it all went wrong.

No surprises that the bank sales executives had no qualms about letting new prospects know (off the record of course) that the Meads had a foreign currency loan with them, as a sweetener to sign other new prospects up to the scam.

The hype applied to sell the foreign currency loans was just as glossy as the Finance Company advertising was and very reminiscent of how the UK Post Office had recruited prospects to take up the Sub Postmaster roles when they glowingly told them that the association with them would be just like a cosy partnership.

During the GFC, the NZ Herald headlined, "Star power behind finance companies" when reporting: "Colin 'Pine Tree" Meads backed Provincial Finance". While another high profile figure, TV news reader Richard Long had also been recruited to front the Hanover Finance advertising program, depicting the security of longevity of the company.

However when it all went pear shaped there was a lot of public blame put on people like the Meads and Richard Long for their part, but in reality they were only following the script given to them and shooting the messenger never helps the situation, which in these cases was futile because when the finance companies knew they were getting into trouble, they quickly used the old Ponzi practice of getting more investors in to pay the bills, therefore it was no accident that they made crafty efforts to score people like the Meads and Richard Long to hide the charade they were playing to bring the new investors in.

In most cases the high flying Finance Company promoters who were pushing the game were the first ones to take their highly inflated fees out.

Fiddling as the ship went down could be said.

It is safe to say that the process is much the same when corporates recruit high profile individuals to sit on their board of directors, whereby a major consideration is given to the profile of individuals to be appointed to the board with the express objective to appease their shareholders and to encourage new people to invest in the company on the share markets in order to keep their share prices high.

Executive bonuses are often pegged to share market results.

The problem is that when high profile individuals take on the responsibility as a company director they are completely reliant on the accuracy of the information they are given in relation to the company's business activities, and given the well noted culture within the corporate world all too often that information has been framed with obscure creative accounting systems in order to keep the board on side.

Maybe that is what happened to the Directors of Mainzeal.

Kneading of the facts about the Post Office's business activities, at the time it was being floated on the stock exchange, has been a dominant revelation in the questioning of Ex Post Office CEO Paula Vennells at the UK inquiry.

The tragedy to justice was that as the finance companies were failing at the rate of about one a week and people's savings were being thrown down the toilet, the Helen Clark Government refused to take any action to protect the investors. Unfortunately the Government were too easily influenced by the high flying directors who blocked any official intervention that may have at least protected some of the people's money from being squandered.

The Government did nothing!

During the 2008-2009 finance companies collapse the support organisation Exposing Unacceptable Financial Activities (EUFA) worked very hard to insist that the Government should set up a Royal Commission of inquiry into the practices of Finance Companies that were causing huge damage to good people of whom many were elderly.

Unfortunately the numbers were so high that the politicians couldn't cope with it and failed to understand that every dollar that could be protected meant a lot to the individual investors, but they simply threw their hands up in the air and blamed the investors for being financially illiterate and greedy.

EUFA had a very chilled meeting with the Commissioner for the elderly when she went on about the need for an education program to make the elderly more financially literate.

The Securities Commission completely refused to take any responsibility and argued with EUFA that the investors deserved to lose their savings because they had been too greedy. They should have been prosecuted for their culpability for the reckless practices they permitted to continue in high flying companies like Bridge Corp that went down and lost many hundred millions of the people's savings.

While the financial calamity was raging Finance Company executives and company directors took drastic actions to cover up their own failings as the companies were going down like skittles. EUFA's investigations identified that in many cases the management had squandered millions of investor's savings, while they continued to draw high fees and perks for themselves. Excessively expensive cars, boats, houses and high living were common.

The record shows that some actions taken by directors and managers were illegal and a few were actually prosecuted, but mostly there was no redress for the public who lost their savings and the lost money just disappeared, probably straight into the pockets of the unseen corporates behind the scenes off shore.

As said, the Governments approach to the situation was that the investors were greedy and needed to be educated to be more financially literate, and strongly opposed the call for the Royal Commission of inquiry that had been presented to a Select Committee hearing at Parliament.

It is amazing that the Forex style scams have continued to be set up as Ponzi schemes to rip people off over the years since, but fortunately the Financial Markets Authority and the Serious Fraud Office have intercepted and arrested some such scams.

One example that raises some interest was exposed in 2019 when the Finance Markets Authority picked up on a scam that they handed over to the Serious Fraud Office who then prosecuted a Foreign exchange broker Kelvin Wood who was sentenced to six years jail.

Unfortunately there was never a thorough forensic investigation into the way the Banks were structuring the foreign currency loans in the 1980's, particularly when it was established that the loans didn't actually exist, because there was no competent compliance enforcement at the time that would investigate the practices being employed by the banking industry. With the frenzy that arose when the loans fell over, it is most likely that the schemes the bankers were peddling were also based on Ponzi principles like the forex scams prosecuted by the Serious Fraud Office in recent times.

It might just be a coincidence that Kelvin Wood is an ex banker, but when the bankers did ruin many good people with their phoney foreign currency scheme in the 1980's, not one of the crooks involved was prosecuted, but many of the victims of their crimes went to their graves having suffered years of the crushing pain and depression from the injustice they had endured.

Chapter 12

Dysfunctional Government desperation.

A letter that was written to the Chief Human Rights Commissioner in 2002 that smells of total confusion, frustration and desperation.

The letter did lead to a meeting with the Chief Commissioner in the Wellington office at which time they were able to show some of the pivotal evidence of the complaint with the BNZ to the two commissioners in attendance.

Dear Ms Noonan

Thank you for your letter of 3rd April 2002.

It is sad to find you have misunderstood the gravity of the oppression inflicted on me that provoked this last resort plea for protection, by the rule of law.

New Zealand is signatory to the 1948 Universal Declaration of Human Rights which states: "Whereas it is essential, if man is not compelled to have recourse, as a last resort, to rebellion against tyranny and oppression, that human rights should be protected by the rule of law,.."

In fairness, I realize you could not be aware of the enormity of the efforts I have already made seeking my rights to be heard through normal commercial, legal and Government authorities prior to contacting your commission, therefore I must advise you of the following facts which will help you understand how your shelving my call may well be the last straw.

Encompassed in a mountain of 2 way correspondence and documented information that evidence details of contact made by me as an individual and in conjunction with others, to no less than the following individuals, organisations and bodies with the express purpose of being awarded a just and fair hearing of the facts that, to my belief, vindicate my position.

Parties involved include:

- *BNZ Management (all levels)*
- *BNZ Board of Directors (all Directors)*
- *BNZ CEO Mike Pratt*
- *BNZ CEO Peter Thodey*
- *Deloitte Touche Tohmatsu John Hager (Receiver)*
- *National Australia bank (Including letter from undersecretary of Revenue)*
- *Banking Ombudsman (Meetings)*
- *Banking Ombudsman Commission*
- *Commerce Commission*

- *Bankers Association*
- *Consumers Institute*
- *Governor of the Reserve Bank Dr Don Brash*
- *Deputy Governor Reserve Bank Dr Rod Carr (Meeting)*
- *New Zealand Prime Minister Rt Hon Mrs Shipley (Meeting)*
- *New Zealand Prime Minister Rt Hon Ms Clark*
- *New Zealand Deputy Prime Minister Rt Hon Jim Anderton*
- *New Zealand Minister of Finance Rt Hoh Sir William Birch*
- *New Zealand Minister of Finance Hon Dr Michael Cullen*
- *New Zealand Minister of Commerce Hon Max Bradford (Meeting)*
- *New Zealand Minister of Commerce Hon Paul Swain (Meeting)*
- *New Zealand Treasurer Rt Hon Winston Peters (Meetings)*
- *New Zealand Minister of Consumer Affairs Hon Phillida Bunkle (Meetings)*
- *New Zealand Minister of Consumer Affairs Hon Peter McCardle*
- *Past New Zealand Minister of Consumer Affairs Hon Katherine O'Regan (Meetings)*

- *New Zealand Minister of Justice Hon Tony Ryall (Meeting)*
- *New Zealand Minister of Justice Hon Phil Goff*
- *Undersecretary of Revenue John Wright MP (Meetings)*
- *High Court of New Zealand Greymouth*
- *High Court of New Zealand Wellington*
- *High Court of New Zealand Christchurch*
- *Several Solicitors and Barristers of the High Court*
- *New Zealand Police*
- *Serious fraud Office*
- *Companies Office*
- *The Speaker of the House of Representatives Hon Jonathan Hunt*
- *The Attorney-General of New Zealand Hon Margaret Wilson*
- *Governor of New Zealand Sir Michael Hardy-Boys*
- *The Governor-General Dame Sylvia Cartwright*
- *The Solicitor-General Terrance Arnold*
- *The Chief Justice Dame Sian Elias*
- *Numerous Members of the New Zealand Parliament (Meetings held with many)*
- *Peter Harris (adviser to Minister of Finance (Meeting)*
- *Departmental Officials (Meetings)*

Although you may think that my laying down the above list in this way is verging on the ridiculous, you must agree, it makes graphic the comprehensive efforts that have been made. The file of documents and information generated by the above contact is impressive. BUT not one person has said that there is no case; they just say "not me". They say, "You are right BUT you can't fight a bank".

A prime example was Mrs Shipley who recently said to my wife and I, in person at Parliament, Quote "I am sorry we didn't do anything at the time (i.e. when she was Prime Minister) but I will do my best to help as much as I can before I leave, as this did happen on my watch". In the enclosed <u>example</u> the Banking Ombudsman stated "The bank expects you to make final submissions......by 30th September 1998...."
While in agreement and support of the validity of my claim several others pleaded to the higher management of BNZ to meet with me.
BUT
There has been no hearing, no submissions viewed and no justice, to this day. Consequently this individual New Zealander was subjected to the loss of my entire property at the hands of the Bank of New Zealand, irrespective of the fact that it was errors of the Bank's systems that led to the situation whereby

they could take action against me in the first place. The simplicity of this matter is that I paid with all I owned, because an individual officer within the bank chose to protect his own position at my expense. (See Parliamentary Hansard Re Farm Debt Mediation Bill debate 31st March 1999. Hon Katherine O'Regan.)

In your letter you suggest I should go to the Courts, but this is unthinkable advice which in itself reiterates the basis of my complaint to you, relating to the purpose of the Human Rights Act. The most draconian power has been bought down on me because money power has taken priority over common justice. Under the force of that power I have been entrapped in an impossible situation. The practices followed under the power of money have actually been enforced to override my natural rights, which is in fact the case I bring. High Court Master Thomas's judgement on the hearing 23rd June 1999 states "…I find that the factual issues involved just cannot be resolved without hearing the witnesses and there being cross examined"…"
BUT, the power of the BNZ's money and the manipulation of the High Court by their lawyers directly corrupted this judgment, ensuring that no

factual issues or witnesses have ever been heard by the High Court.

Given the magnitude of my efforts, all of which have been deemed "too hard", it has to be concluded that it would be totally reasonable to describe my position as that of a man compelled to have recourse by rebellion. Accordingly, I ask you as Chief Commissioner, by what form the General Assembly might have expected such rebellion to be manifested under such circumstances.

As a person with considerable personal credibility, I am one New Zealander who has made a larger that normal contribution to my country and during my life spanning 53 years have never been charged with, nor have I ever committed a crime, but the human rights universally awarded to me have been denied, whereas the BNZ has been permitted, in full view of the authorities involved, to override natural justice by inflicting the oppressive power of its money.

In view of the personal degradation I have endured, it may be fair to argue under the Universal Declaration of Human Rights that I have been denied protection from oppression by the rule of law, as promised, thus,

It's now 2024 and 22 years have now passed since this desperate letter was written and the BNZ has simply got away with it.

The amounts of money that were stolen from unsuspecting customers will never be known.

But, where was the State in all this?

The Ministers of the Government don't care; the end result is that a bank can steal money if it wants to and there is no law enforcement available in New Zealand to deliver the law and bring prosecutions.

As it transpires the Chief Human Rights Commissioner hasn't got any powers of enforcement to uphold the Universal Declaration of Human Rights as most people would rightly expect they would.

The Eatwells thought that was the purpose of the office as most people would.

That is unless you have a complaint that involves an ism of course.

When the Eatwells took their well-founded complaints to Parliament they were repeatedly sent to the Banking Ombudsman, but when the Banking Ombudsman Commission was questioned about its Human Rights status, in response to the Eatwells question to the Chairman Ron Paterson, he replied 8 April 2011:

Dear Mr Eatwell

"You have asked me to confirm that the Banking Ombudsman Scheme is now responsible for upholding the state's obligations to honour the conditions of the Universal Declaration of Human Rights.

While the Banking Ombudsman Scheme has obtained Ministerial approval under the Financial Service Providers (Registration and Dispute Resolution) Act 2008, it continues to operate under independent governance. As previously advised, it is not a tribunal of the sort envisaged by the Universal Declaration of Human Rights.

The Banking Ombudsman Scheme is therefore not responsible for upholding the States obligations under the various human rights instruments.

Yours sincerely

Professor Ron Paterson"

Universal Declaration of Human Rights:

Article 8.

Everyone has the right to an effective remedy by the competent national tribunal for acts violating the fundamental rights granted to him by the constitution or by law.

In this age of political correctness that actually comes from the founding document the Universal Declaration of Human Rights, signatory States Government Politicians have concentrated on splinter rights or extreme individual rights and failed dismally in their obligations to deliver the basic right to citizens to be protected from oppression by the rule of law especially when a big corporate is involved.

There has been no "competent national tribunal" to provide an effective remedy for the Eatwells for the acts of the BNZ that have violated their fundamental rights that has definitely oppressed them.

Rosslyn Noonan advised Hon Peter Dunne that the obligation to uphold the International Human Rights law is that of the State, represented by the elected Government, but the elected Government believes that by setting up commissions like the Human Rights Commission, and leaning on the industry funded Banking Ombudsman, it has unthinkingly given them a flawed belief that they have satisfied their obligations to International Human Rights laws.

Even the Governor General Sir Michael Hardy- Boys advised that *"Regulations relating to the operations of banks are the responsibility of Government Ministers"*

After Dame Sylvia Cartwright was sworn as Governor General in 2001 there was a chain of correspondence reporting the States systems were failing to provide the fundamental right to an effective remedy for the disputes with Banks in New Zealand, in which Dame Sylvia gave similar advice that Sir Michael Hardy- Boys had, but the essence of the advice given was that the issues that were presented to them as the Head of State's representatives was that Justice must be made available by the Government.

Given the legal background of the Governor Generals involved and Dame Sylvia's Human Rights interests her attention to the matter of injustice being pleaded was taken seriously.

Maybe Governor-Generals are only seen as figureheads, but they did represent the Head of State, Queen Elizabeth 11 at that time and both of the Governors that we communicated with had considerable credibility of high level legal backgrounds.

But in reality the correspondence actually amounted to "No Not me Guv"

But, a letter from the Attorney-General Hon Margaret Wilson followed being advised of the impossible recommendation to the Eatwell petitions from the Select Committee; she wrote:

"This seems to me to be the appropriate approach. I understand from the Committee's report that the Banking Ombudsman is prepared to assist you further. Your complaints with the BNZ are matters to be taken up with the Banking Ombudsman."

As Lord James Arbuthnot told the inquiry into the UK Post Office scandal about the Corporate executives being questioned, that there is a "No not me Guv" theme to their responses.

Maybe that's what the Attorney General also meant to say. "No not me Guv"

Obviously it is way past time that politicians elected to Parliament woke up to the fact that they have the express responsibility to uphold the international standards of obligations to which the State of New Zealand is a signatory.

If you are a sworn member of the legislature of New Zealand, that is you "Guv".

As said, there have been many elected Members of the New Zealand Parliament involved with the Eatwell case, and with the many other people the Bank Customer Action Collective have advocated for. Gray and Vickie Eatwell have travelled the length and breadth of New Zealand meeting many good people who have been savaged by the banking Industry's draconian debt recovery tactics.

Frequently actions taken by banks flout the insolvency laws, but no one in authority ever challenges the legality of the doubtful processes applied and "they get away with it".

"The baddies get off scot free"

The insolvency laws are effectively used as a weapon by the bankers and their lawyers and fail to observe the fundamental Human Rights obligations of all Acts of Parliament.

There were some Members of Parliament and others who have tried very hard to achieve fairness for victims of the actions imposed on bank customers, but they have all been shot down and/or shut down or misled. Mainly by their own political parties, others by the pressure of the bankers, therefore watching the UK Post Office scandal inquiry progress, it is hard not to respect Lord James Arbuthnot (Ex-British MP) in his selfless stand demanding justice for the victims of the corporate brutality he has witnessed to his horror, in his own homeland.

The Eatwells and many of the people whom they have met in their own kitchens in their farm houses, or work smoko rooms when they were totally broken by their bankers and some-times suicidal; they can only wish for another Lord James Arbuthnot to appear in the New Zealand Parliament in 2024.

Those NZ MP's (those who are still with us and those who have sadly passed on), who have tried to help bank customers being oppressed are very much appreciated, but the dysfunctional Parliamentary system has proven to be too hard for them to penetrate and even to understand in some cases.

Unfortunately facts recorded in "The Labyrinth of Deceit and Betrayal" have exposed the unhealthy truth that the New Zealand Government is caught up in systems that have become deficient in the ability to comply with International Human Rights laws, accordingly, the legislature is unable to deliver the fundamental obligations of State.

Boy oh boy, there has been so much "No not me Guv" flying around New Zealand's Parliament in this story that the conclusion must be that the dysfunction up at Parliament has caused the State to commit crimes against International Human Rights laws.

The question posed to the Chief Commissioner in the above letter was," *By what form the General-Assembly might have expected such rebellion to be manifested under such circumstances".*

There was no specific and or helpful answer from the Human Rights Commission.

However from the experience of meeting many individuals in the grip of deep depression that overpowers a person suffering gross injustice imposed on them by corporate hands; it can be concluded that it is only by the good nature of the person being a hard working law abiding citizen, who would not harm others, that the rebellion is all too often manifested by the act of suicide.

Sadly, all too often when a man thinks he is losing the family farm the shame and feelings of failure is too much to take. The ramifications to their lives are severe.

In many situations the natural impulse is to fight back violently which causes a rage of confusion that manifests as a state of panic in many people.

In the book "You can Bank on it" it is written about the confusion a person feels when the corporate axe comes down on them, sighting the time when the police were sent to the Eatwells farm at Franz Josef to evict them. In this event Gray Eatwell confessed to his fear of panic, saying, "*I still feel cold when I think of how little it would have taken to break the twig that day*".

"Although this memory still sickens me, I am so thankful for everyone's sake, and in particular the families of the police personnel sent down that day – it was not their fault but is was their lives on the line."

With the knowledge of Gray Eatwell's background as a professional meat hunter back in the 1970's, Ian Wishart wrote in the first edition of his book "Daylight Robbery" "hell this could be Aramoana all over again."

"This guy could shoot".

It is during a state of panic that the feelings of helplessness, desperate thoughts can also cause suicide to be a real option to a confused mind.

In "You can Bank on it" it is also written that *"Suicide is a mental torture and the trap is real.*

Obviously I am not a fatality, but I am definitely a victim of the mental disease, suicide."

In recent times there was a situation that involved Gray and Vickie Eatwell when a friend in the North Island rang Gray saying, "there is a bloke down your way that I am very worried about. He is under the pump from his bank and I am scared that he is going to shoot someone, most likely himself".

This man had also been involved with the helicopter deer recovery industry in his earlier days.

The Eatwells had become friends with the caller when he and his family were booted off their farm some years before, so they knew he wouldn't exaggerate such a serious situation, so they took him at his word and made tracks immediately.

They quickly drove to the man's farm, one and a half hours away and arrived at a very solemn cold looking place. With huge relief they found the man in a bad state of depression, but still living. It took a long time, but his mood slowly improved.

"Did you think you would find me hanging from the rafters" he said.

 "Yes, we were scared that might be what we would find, or maybe worse" was their answer.

The Eatwells did go to other people in the same depressed situations, or when people were rapidly heading towards it, over the years.

It really hurts, but to be able to help people climb out of the deepest depression imposed on them, because they know you really do understand how they feel, is so worth the pain it takes.

A real human manifestation of being a *"last resort to, rebellion against tyranny and oppression, that human rights should be protected by the rule of law..."*

In New Zealand, when you are up against a bank the rule of common law is forgotten.

As it is being exposed in the UK Post Office scandal that the longer a miscarriage of justice is imposed on people, it is the longer they suffer the feelings of debilitation.

As the pain continues, the State of New Zealand's failure to uphold the rule of law is not only a crime against the General Assembly Human Rights Council; it is a crime against the people of New Zealand.

At this time in 2024 the foreign owned banks are squeezing their parameters around struggling farmers and other small to medium business people in New Zealand, using their own practices invented to let them charge excess interest rates and altering a person's debt to equity ratios by down valuing their assets to the so called fire sale values and low ball land values.

Shifting the goal posts to claim risk to the bank and charge more interest.

Next move is insolvency.

In the name of the State of New Zealand the Government had better wake up to their responsibility as the guardians of the Human Rights laws that do not have a price tag.

We all have the right to be protected from oppression and the methods applied by the banking industry are definitely very oppressive.

Chapter 13

A labyrinth, spiral or nightmare?

This story is not about how the State's Human Rights obligations have been omitted, it is more likely that the Legislature deliberately (and/or negligently) obstructed any possibility of the deliverance of a just hearing for the Eatwell Vs BNZ case.

The Eatwells had opened a can of worms that exposed crimes of a major NZ bank.

From the highest level of Government false excuses were contrived to divert the obligations of the legislature to provide the basic rights that were being pleaded.

For Example:

31st March 1999: In the Farm Debt Mediation debate John Wright MP told the House "But farmers should not be put in the position of Mr Eatwell of Franz Josef whose property has been mentioned here tonight, who for months went from the Banking Ombudsman, to the Bank, to all other sources , seeking satisfaction. He has a letter from the Banking Ombudsman saying: 'There are problems here that have not been resolved, but the bank does not appear to want to resolve them'.

From that time forward the Banking Ombudsman was not able to assist the Eatwells at all, and Mrs Brown said so.

However the pertinent point being that the Banking Ombudsman never indicated that the Eatwells had no case for the bank to answer. She saw enough to know there was a real issue to be heard.

Eventually the Eatwells were advised to petition Parliament which they did on more than one occasion, with the result being that the Select Committee, the Prime Minister, Attorney General and Parliamentary officials kept telling the Eatwells to take their case to the Banking Ombudsman.

At the first petition (the only time a hearing was held) the Select Committee were supplied with letters from the Banking Ombudsman: E.g. 16th May 2002 Stating "…there is nothing to change the view I have already expressed to you, which is that there is no further action that can be taken through my office……."

BUT, the Select Committee's official recommendation stated: We ask that the Banking Ombudsman work in a meaningful manner with Mr Eatwell with a view to resolve his concerns…"

30th April 2004 the Attorney –General advised "… I understand from the Committees report that the Banking Ombudsman is prepared to assist you further."

Then they decided to block the case by claiming that all; courses of action had not been exhausted.

19th May 2004 Tim Barnett MP chairman of the Select Committee wrote to Liz Brown suggesting to her that the Eatwells had not exhausted their options "…. In relation to the Banking Ombudsman,"

3rd June 2004 the Attorney-General wrote: "Your petition to Parliament was heard despite the fact that you had not exhausted all you're available legal remedies. The Justice and Electoral Committee, which heard your petition, suggested you work with the Banking Ombudsman to resolve your concerns."

The day before, the 2nd June 2004 the Banking Ombudsman had written Mr Eatwell a comprehensive letter including "After reading the Select Committee report, I was somewhat concerned at its recommendation; I therefore sought a meeting with Mr Tim Barnett MP …."

In the fourth paragraph she said: "I explained to Mr Barnett, as I have explained to you in the past……………."I could see virtually no possibility of re-opening my investigation of your complaint."

The parliamentary systems continued to block the Eatwell's efforts to be taken seriously to the point that the when Hon Peter Dunne kept trying to plead with the Parliament to do its job, he received a letter from the Clerk of the House of Representatives: 20th October 2004 stating : "The Banking Ombudsman may still find in favour of Mr Eatwell,…."

In response to the Clerk's statement that was obviously total wrong on 4th November 2004 The Banking Ombudsman wrote directly to Mr Botar Parliamentary Officer: Mr Eatwell has sent me a copy of your memorandum of 20 October 2004 sent to the Hon Peter Dunne and asked me to confirm to you that there is no possibility of progressing his complaint through the Banking Ombudsman process."

The Banking Ombudsman had been saying the same thing since 1998.

The circle continued, but the result of the Irish High Court investigation into the BNZ's sister bank had been published in July 2004, but in total denial of the facts before it the State of New Zealand was obviously not going to uphold its International Human Rights law obligations to the people of New Zealand as the Irish Government had.

The end result has to be that the disgusting experience has been a mind spinning nightmare.

Banking Ombudsman

Chapter 14

Citizen's rights grossly overstated.

The UK Post Office scandal inquiry has heard from many witnesses who have told the inquiry a number of tactics they encountered from the Post Office and their lawyers have direct parallels to the Eatwell case and otheres in New Zealand.

Sir Alan Bates told the inquiry that the practices applied against sub Postmasters was totally unacceptable:

Tantamount to: in the 60 minutes Documentary David Russell of the Consumer, (a member of the Banking Ombudsman Commission) that the actions of the BNZ were "totally unacceptable" particularly by taking action to bankrupt the Eatwells in disregard of a complaint being investigated by the Banking Ombudsman.

Ron Warrington from Second Sight told the UK inquiry that documents had been withheld and/or redacted and destroyed.

Tantamount to: When the Eatwells requested documents from the BNZ they refused to provide the documents forcing the Eatwells to go to the Privacy Commissioner who then instructed the bank to supply them.

It took a face to face with the Commissioner to get action but eventually the Privacy Commission contacted the Eatwells and said they had a parcel of documents that had been delivered to their office by hand from the BNZ. So as they would be in Wellington the next week the Eatwells arranged to go up to the Privacy Commission's office to collect the information.

On arriving at the office they were presented with a medium sized carton full of documents with the throw away quip that it was just like the wine box episode in the House of Parliament, quite some years earlier.

Damn, it wasn't a wine box, it was a biscuit box (about the same size though).

The box was full of some heavily redacted documents and some that must have slipped through their system or else the banker had run out of time or black marker ink.

The redaction gave the appearance of how a child would busily black out most of the content on some of the documents, but with a bit of light exposure most of the content was still visible.

Parliamentary officials withheld crucial documents from the Select Committee dealing with the Eatwell petitions to parliament seeking an effective remedy for the denial of a just hearing in the case of malpractice imposed by the BNZ, as a consequence Prime Minister and senior Cabinet Ministers summations of the Eatwell case based on the petitions were ultra vires, therefore the decisions made at the top level of Government were in breach of Ministry of Justice ruling that Members of Parliament are obligated to ensure decisions they make are accurate and fair.

Ian Henderson of Second Sight: Forensic accountant explained to the inquiry how the Post Office lawyers had threatened Second Sight with action that could bankrupt them if they exposed the truth about the actions made against the sub Postmasters. He spoke of threats and blackmail the same as David Russell had said in the 60 Minutes Documentary.

Tantamount to: The BNZ took bankruptcy actions against the Eatwells to shut down the High Court claim they had lodged.

The banks lawyer had drawn up a document offering a real low ball settlement arrangement that was pivotal on the Eatwells signing a silencing agreement along with demands that any family member or associate of the Eatwells could never enter a BNZ branch, communicate with the bank or make any public statement about the bank.

The draconian demands of the document were the subject of a law Society complaint relating to common law rights that the document had breached.

The Law Society did nothing of course.

Paula Vennells Ex CEO UK Post Office: In Ms Vennells earlier approach to the inquiry was that of self-pity and apology. She claimed she never knew what was going on and that her staff had misled her. As the questioning continued a different picture has emerged that has proven that Ms Vennells had known about the sub Postmaster prosecutions and the IT system failures relatively early in the piece.

Tantamount to: From 1998 the CEO of the BNZ the CEO of National Australia Bank (the owner of BNZ) Every director on the BNZ board of Directors were all advised that Bank of New Zealand Limited had overcharged the Eatwell companies business accounts, with pleadings for remedial action.

The pleadings were repeated in 2004 following the Irish High Court report exposing the same practice being applied at the Nab owned National Irish Bank. The Irish High Court report explained in detail how the illegal charges were applied in Ireland detailing the process that shows the results recorded by the Eatwells as being identical in their delivery.

The fact that one of the Directors of the BNZ was Pamela Jefferies who had been the Chief Human Rights Commissioner was very hard to reconcile.

Irrespective of the trauma the Eatwell family endured from being made to be destitute, the only response received was the inaccurate written statement that was shown at the end of the TVNZ 60 Minutes Documentary.

-

There are a number of parallels to the UK Post Office revelations recorded in this book, but the observation has revealed a very serious threat to the degradation of the true value of International Human Rights Laws to which our free counties are signatory to at the United Nations.

Whitehall in the UK was made aware of the travesty of sub Postmasters being persecuted based on a faulty IT system as early as 2009 or maybe before, but the UK Government totally ignored the States obligations to which they have the duty to uphold.

Tantamount to: The State of New Zealand was advised that a bank registered by the Reserve Bank of New Zealand under statutory conditions, had allegedly taken illegal action against a customer and had ignored the Banking Ombudsman's judgment.

The allegation was subsequently proven by fact and presented to Government at every level as it is recorded in this book.

Sir Alan Bates has also told media that he is concerned about the delay in compensating the victims of the "Greatest miscarriage of Justice in the legal history of the UK" and he has observed the bureaucratic machine impacting on the desperate needs of the victims who have had more than 20 years of their lives destroyed, not to make light of those who couldn't cope and committed suicide.

In New Zealand there has been no inquiry but Sir Alan Bates is not necessarily being paranoid, particularly as the UK betrayal of Human Rights is following New Zealand's example of the Human Rights betrayal.

Recommendations from the United Nations led to the NZ Government establishing the Waitangi Tribunal back in 1975.

In the UK an empire has been built by the Boffins to administer the compensation of the victims of the Post

Office dishonesty, but as usual this process looks like it will take forever to reach a just result, so let's hope it doesn't mirror the NZ example of Human Rights deliverance.

Slow justice is no justice. It has taken a beleaguered ex-employee of the BNZ who reported serious wrong doings at the bank 8 years to be afforded a judgement in June 2024.

This may be seen as a long bow to draw, but the way it is grinding on in Westminster and with the high handed low ball offers being made by officials designed to get rid of the claimants; Sir Alan has every right to be concerned at the process becoming a marathon on top of the triathlon and summiting Everest he and his group have endured.

In July 2006 Hon Peter Dunne wrote to the Attorney-General about "Mr Eatwell's dilemma" Stating that: "it is questionable whether he has been taken seriously by any of them. He is now left feeling that the entire process is somewhat farcical, and that his rights as a citizen are grossly overstated."

The Attorney-General's reply to Hon Peter Dunne has been established as being ultra vires in its obvious intent which when combined with other Government and Parliamentary inaccuracies has culminated in being a key factor of the deceit that effectively orchestrated the cover-up that caused the betrayal of the deliverance of Mr Eatwells basic rights as citizens of NZ.

The British Commonwealth countries went to war together and it looks like the Governments of the UK and NZ are both going to degrade the sacrifice our forefathers made for us to live in a free and just society by their betrayal of the State.

The United Nations-General Assembly- Human Rights Council- Working Group on the Universal Periodic Review of New Zealand's Human Rights standards made the following judgment and recommendations:

Remedies Compensation and rehabilitation:

"Individuals who consider that any of their rights under the Bill of Rights Act (BORA) have been infringed can bring an action against the Government. A number of remedies are available, including the ability to award damages or compensation.... . "

That must be how a citizen can navigate the farce ("bring action against the Government") and be delivered their grossly overstated rights in this overstated promise of a Free World.

Yeah Right!

On the 26th June 2024 the Employment Relations Authority ruled in favour of Mellissa Bowen in the case vs BNZ that was founded on "serious wrongdoing" she witnessed as a long term employee of the bank and had reported the matter as a Whistle Blower under the Protected Disclosures Act.

Protected, no way, the BNZ began an "orchestrated retaliatory campaign" against Mellissa Bowen which culminated in her being booted out of her job (just like Sir Alan Bates and the Eatwells) rather than investigate and remedy the illegal conduct she had reported.

Mellissa Bowen's complaint had been made with the belief that the Protected Disclosures Act would actually protect her from being persecuted.

Wrong!

In New Zealand foreign owned banks like the BNZ are able to operate above the law of the land and have a well-known corporate culture of villainising any person who dares to complain about the organisation's inherent improprieties.

Obviously any corporate bank (or other corporate) with any integrity would reward employees who did the right thing and reported malpractice they observe in the businesses operations.

Exactly what the reported wrong doing was in this case is unknown, but banks do money- other people's money, so it most likely that the problem is money, and as it involves a senior manager we know from the Irish High Court report that senior managers feature quite a lot doing the Nab's devious work. If it wasn't money directly involved it could be another one of the Nab practices of backstabbing to climb up the corporate ladder and be rewarded with bonuses, as it is prevalent in that corporate.

It has taken 8 years of horrific treatment from the bank, but Mellissa Bowen knew she was right and like Sir Alan Bates she kept fighting the vile culture of the Nab owned corporate bank and at last the Employment Relations Authority have ruled against the "orchestrated retaliatory campaign" the bank has mounted against her.

The only difference between Mellissa Bowen's case and the subject matter of the Eatwell case evidenced in this book is that she saw and reported the illegal practice as an employee of the BNZ and the Eatwells detected the bank's malpractice as customers.

The rest of the ugly "retaliatory campaign" mounted against them was pretty much the same Nab modus operandi as has been the Nab way for no less than the 25 years as it is recorded in this work.

The travesty of this vile culture going unchallenged over the 25 years of the Eatwell case being reported at every level of State is that if the Government had upheld its Human Rights obligations of State, Mellissa Bowen and many other victims of the Australia owned bank would have been spared the trauma suffered at the hands of the executive culture that has been recorded in "Labyrinth of Deceit and Betrayal".

The financial and human cost is unthinkable.

Paul Appleby in Ireland, Charles Sturt ex SFO, Sir Alan Bates, the Supreme Court of New Zealand, The UN Human Rights Committee, and many others have warned of the societal cost of covering-up white collar Crime.

Karl Flinders one of the scandal breaking journalists from the UK Computer Weekly said that, *"it's so frustrating watching those with power and influence trample on people unchallenged …….. Credit should go to the victims and campaigners who fought for justice. It feels surreal what the Post Office tried to do, and they almost got away with it."*

Sadly in New Zealand the BNZ have "got away with it" for 25 years.

They "got off Scot Free", Sir Alan Bates.

The New Zealand legislature (Government) should hang its head in shame.

Epilogue:

Those victims of injustice, simply because they had the courage to try getting ahead in life, have felt the pain of the stress bought down on them by the power of corporate executives, but it is hard to understand what drives the individual executives and officials involved.

The simple answer has to be money, greed and ego.

In most cases the executives who wield the power in big organisations are invariably paid uncouth salaries and bonuses with no performance and/or legal accountability, while small business operators with all of their property on the line normally live below the minimum wage level.

In New Zealand there is no law enforcement available to prosecute white collar crime in the banking industry and executives of other multi-national corporates, so there is a real threat to "Social disruption and economic damage caused".

The moral bar is high to those individuals under oath to the Government/legislature, because it is you who hold the legal obligations of the State of New Zealand.

That is you "Guv".

The Banking Industry and other big Corporates do not have an automatic right to take unearned profit and the people do have a natural right to protection from oppression as promised by the State under international Human Rights Law.

Commercial forces do not provide protection from corporate abuse of financial power.

With Farmers and Business people of New Zealand buckling under the load of high debt levels and high interest charges in 2024, particularly at a time that the profitability of their business is struggling, I implore the Government to get off their party driven high horses and understand the gravity of what it actually means to be sworn as an elected member of the legislature of New Zealand.

The purpose of this work is not a witch hunt, even though there may be some witches and baddies exposed the objective is specifically focused on the truth being recorded.

Even though the reaction expected will be a character assassination and personal degradation of the writer, the truth of the events involved are indisputable.

All claims of deceit being made are specifically directed at
the registered entity Bank of New Zealand Limited and
claims of betrayal of duty to the State are specifically
directed at the entity of the State as represented by the
sworn New Zealand Government, not any particular
individual elected members, political parties or Government
employed officers and/or authorities.

The deceit has been administered by employees and/or
appointed governors of the Bank of New Zealand Limited
and by decisions made on behalf of the State of New Zealand
being ultra vires, constituting a betrayal to the States
obligations to the United Nations International Human Rights
laws.

The recorded facts of the actions made to effect the denials
and betrayal of the State and   citizens' rights may involve
criminality, however the statutory obligation to prosecute
any such crimes falls on the Official Offices of compliance
and the legal system to ensure justice is seen to be delivered
to the people.

Upholding criminal law is not the obligation of the
complainants of the dishonesty involved.

The States deficiencies have been exacerbated by the failure
of the Government to implement recommendations made
by the United Nations working group periodic review

committee to provide effective remedies to persons subjected to oppression, but the UN criticism was treated with distain and/or ho-hum in Wellington.

This top level snubbing of the UN Human Rights committee recommendations has culminated in the betrayal of individuals fundamental rights to justice that are central to the subject.

John Wright MP told the House of Representatives during the Farm Debt Mediation debate: "Fair play should be what this House is about".

If only John.

www.ingramcontent.com/pod-product-compliance
Lightning Source LLC
Chambersburg PA
CBHW051558250726
48653CB00004BA/1210